Getting Organized
in the *Era of Endless*

What to Do When Information, Interruption, Work and Stuff are Endless
But Time is Not!

Judith Kolberg

Published by
Squall Press
P. O. Box 691
Decatur, G.A. 30031
www.squallpress.net
404-231-6172

ISBN: 978-0966797-0-9-1

This book is for informational purposes only. It is sold with the understanding that the publisher and author are not engaged in rendering legal, accounting, financial, or other professional services. If such advice is required, the services of a qualified professional should be sought.

Design by Debbie Kerr

Printed in the United States by
BookLogix, www.booklogix.com

IN PRAISE OF GETTING ORGANIZED IN THE ERA OF ENDLESS

"This book takes organizing into the future based on a historical perspective of organizing. It provides a unique and new perspective on dealing with technology and modern life. Judith offers new solutions to seize control of our ever-expanding technology-driven life and digital endlessness. She brings it back to humanity. A must-read if you want to stay ahead."—Angelique Bouwman, Vice-President of the Association for Dutch Professional Organizers (NBPO)

"Kolberg is the master of observing, understanding, and explaining human behavior as it relates to organization. The *Era of Endless* humorously connects the dots between how people lived and acquired things throughout human history and the organizational systems they created to manage their lives. Most importantly, Judith offers innovative organizing solutions so you and I can get control of the endless stream of information, tasks, and stuff that come into our lives and the lives of our clients."—Katherine Trezise, CPO, CPO-CD, Absolutely Organized, LLC, Past President, Institute for Challenging Disorganization

"In the past couple of decades, our world has been turned upside down by the seemingly endless parade of stuff coming our way. In her book, *The Era of Endless*, Judith Kolberg tackles this topic head-on. She traces the origins of our clutter all the way back to the days of the caveman and brings us up to today's digital domain. Ms Kolberg's insights are spot on, as are her strategies for helping us keep our sanity. I highly recommended this book to anyone trying to stay organized in this new Era of Endless."—Paul O'Connor, Master Certified Coach, Board Member of the Professional Association of ADHD Coaches

"Buy this book—then get rid of a bunch of stuff. Life in the information age requires us to make active choices in the face of a flood of infor-mation and potential obligations. Judith Kolberg will not only explain why you feel overwhelmed (who doesn't?), but will help you make smart decisions about what really deserves your attention. This is my new go-to resource for clients who feel overwhelmed by it all and have lost track of what is most important."—Ari Tuckman, PsyD, MBA, Author, *Understand Your Brain, Get More Done*

"Judith touches all of us personally by showing a historical frame for getting and staying organized. She encourages us to anticipate the barrage of 'stuff' and shows us how to stay ahead of it. Judith's advice is sound with deep emotional understanding."—Krys Moskal-Amdurer, Vice President, Pearson People Development

"As a small business consultant and service provider I can attest that many business problems emanate from lack of organization. In this witty and enjoyable book Judith not only covers the basics, but also pioneers new approaches for managing the 24/7 barrage of information and demands assaulting us in the digital age. I consider *Era of Endless* to be a must-read not only for my clients and Angels, but also for my friends and family. Judith's practical wisdom definitely enhances quality of life."— Essie Escobedo, Chief Executive Angel, Office Angels®

"Judith Kolberg is the most visionary leader in our industry. When she speaks or writes, I go out of my way to listen. *Getting Organized in the Era of Endless* is a superior book."—Dorothy Breininger, Organizing Expert to *Hoarders*, the A&E's Emmy Nominated TV show

"Judith's newest book, *The Era of Endless* is a tour-de-force for the organizing industry. Written with wit and humor, Judith offers a well-researched historical perspective of our relationship to getting organized. A thought-leader in the organizing industry, Judith presents her unique spin and meaningful solutions. The Era of Endless is original and a must-read for anyone interested in where we have been and where we are going with regard to organizing and productivity."—Lisa Montanaro, author, *The Ultimate Life Organizer: An Interactive Guide to a Simpler, Less Stressful & More Organized Life.*

"Kolberg is a pioneer and thought-leader in the organizing industry. In her latest book, *Getting Organized in the Era of Endless*, she uses a historical and socio-cultural lens to reveal the interconnected complexities arising from having everything available anytime at the touch of our fingers. The result is a rich read that is intuitive, humorous, and thought-provoking for consumers and audiences from multiple backgrounds who are besieged by information, choices, stuff, and distractions—and who struggle to manage the only finite resource—time."—Catherine A. Roster, Ph.D., Associate Professor, Anderson School of Management, The University of New Mexico

"Judith Kolberg's insights are must-reads for anyone seeking to adapt their personal and work lives to our changing times. *The Era of Endless* offers a fascinating ride through history as viewed through the prism of getting organized. Kolberg provides clear strategies for coping and succeeding in today's world with the advent of endless everything, now that historical methods have become outdated."—Stephanie Denton, author, *The Organized Life: Secrets of an Expert Organizer*

"Judith Kolberg strikes a nerve in this enlightening book. As a busy executive and personal coach, I know we all can suffer from the syndrome of 'too much muchness.' Kolberg comes to our rescue by giving us a solid understanding of how this Era of Endless happened. Plus, she provides concrete ideas on how to allocate our time as we divide and conquer the endless streams of information, interruptions, work, and stuff."
—Jane McMullan Howe, Executive and Personal Coach, Ed.S., ACC

"Scratch the surface of Judith Kolberg's delightful and witty style, and you'll find the depth of research and scrutiny of a scholar, matched with ardent curiosity: Where did that term come from? How did that concept evolve? How is this connected to that?—questions you almost hear her asking on every page. She dives deeply into the organizing issues of modern living and continues to set the bar for our industry. A fun and enlightening read!"—Jocelyn Coverdale, President Ballantrae Solutions

"Judith Kolberg is a pioneer in the Professional Organizing field and visionary for its future. In *The Era of Endless*, she analyzes the development of organizing skills in the context of the past and offers a new paradigm for the future. If Kolberg writes it, I will read it and learn from it, and this book is no exception."—Casey Moore, The Productivity Coach, author, *Stop Organizing, Start Producing*

"I am excited about Judith Kolberg's new book, *The Era of Endless*. Judith points out what makes it hard for us to get organized in our busy, high tech world. She then makes simple and effective suggestions to manage our lives and our stuff. Most interestingly, Judith begins with a brief history of how early humans were the first 'organizers' and shows how the need for organizing has increased throughout history. We need professional organizers like Judith to help us use our limited time to keep our lives in order."—Herb Bastin, Owner, Bastin Media Technical Service

ACKNOWLEDGEMENTS

I would like to express a special thanks to the many people who made this book possible. Debbie Kerr's commitment, creativity, and careful attention to detail are much appreciated. Julie Bestry provided excellent research. Francis Wade is an experimenter like me and a source of inspiration. My Mom, Linda McGuire, Tami Puckett, and Clara Welch were always in my court. Melissa Mannon contributed valuable information. A special shout-out to the NAPO Tech SIG, especially Jocelyn Coverdale, Karen Simon, and Alix Longfellow. Jessica Parker at BookLogix is a gem. Thank goodness Lori Vande Krol has her head in the cloud. Thanks also to the Lamers family, Ine, Thijs, Marieke, Daan, Bas, and Frans (and Uncle Frans) for their hospitality, fun, and support exactly when I needed it most.

TABLE OF CONTENTS

Part Four:
What To Do When Interruption is Endless and Time is Not............... 87

FOREWORD

When I met Judith Kolberg I had no idea who she was. I had just arrived at the 2012 annual Institute for Challenging Disorganization Conference in Chicago to a ballroom filled with 200 professional organizers, my audience for an upcoming speech. I had little idea what to expect as I drifted over to the safety of the snack table. Before I had a chance to fill my plate, a rather short woman approached me. She introduced herself as Judith Kolberg and asked what I'd be talking about. I gave her a very general overview and a vague smile, only to discover that I had made a mistake. She wasn't just making idle chit-chat near the hors d'oeuvres. Instead, 20 minutes later, my tired mind was spinning: I could barely keep up with her questions. They were well-formed and she had strong points of view on my area of expertise, time management. Luckily, we seemed to agree on most things and when someone pulled her away I was a bit relieved. If every attendee in this conference was just as informed, I'd need to spend a lot more time working on my presentation.

A day later, I discovered that she wasn't an average attendee. I had been speaking with a giant: not in physical terms, but in stature. When I later read her first book, *Conquering Chronic Disorganization*, I came to understand the pioneering role she played in the industry of professional organizing. Her ideas represented a clear and defining breakthrough in thinking.

This book, *Getting Organized in the Era of Endless: What To Do When Information, Interruption, Work and Stuff are Endless and Time is Not*, fills another gaping hole in our understanding. Her multi-generational story that begins with a cave-woman and ends with a modern-day couple shows us the human yen to be organized; first in order to survive and then in order to make the most of life.

Today, however, things are different. We have exactly the same amount of time to get everything done, but we live in an ocean of information that we cannot control, only filter. Thanks to the latest technology, we must allocate our attention 24 hours a day, 7 days a week. We are an open channel for interruptions, messages, requests, reminders, news updates, and more. It's all become inescapable, yet irresistible. The Era of Endless is upon us and it promises more information delivered faster than ever. Some would look at this as an unplanned disaster, but Kolberg takes the archeologist's point of view—her book presents the facts as they appear to the eye of a highly trained professional organizer. This is where *Getting Organized in the Era of Endless* excels.

Kolberg's understanding of the big picture shows us how to discern this "ocean" in terms of its awesome demands on our time. Furthermore, she teaches us ways to shape our lives to remain productive in spite of the unprecedented volume of stuff we must deal with. This book represents a big step in giving us the knowledge we need to live life fully. She makes it clear that we must contend with its onslaught if we hope to go beyond survival to success. I am so glad I met Judith and came to know her through her ideas.

Francis Wade
Consultant and Author,
Bill's Imperfect Time Management Adventure

INTRODUCTION

There are many ways to describe what it means to get organized. "Organizing is the process by which we create environments that enable us to live, work, and relax exactly as we want to. When we are organized, our homes, offices and schedules reflect and encourage who we are, what we want, and where we are going," eloquently states Julie Morgenstern, in her book, *Organizing From the Inside Out.* Barry Izsak, a former President of the National Association of Professional Organizers (NAPO) describes getting organized this way: "Organization is a valuable component of a fully realized life, integral to personal productivity and professional success."

No matter how it is defined, getting organized allows us to enjoy a better quality of life. 71% of respondents to a 2012 survey conducted by NAPO indicated their quality of life would improve with more organization.[1] Because getting organized is so strongly tied to quality of life, it has remained among the top ten New Years' resolutions for two decades.[2]

I've been privileged, as a public speaker, to travel to Japan and The Netherlands. I've had organizing clients in Bermuda and Costa Rica. And I've corresponded regularly with readers of my organizing books in Korea, Brussels, England, and Saudi Arabia. Everyone I've spoken with shares the view that quality of life and organization are paired. "Professional organizers are uniquely able to influence a client on reaching goals, managing stress, and getting things done," notes Mayumi Takahari, President of the Japanese Association of Life Organizers. Reaching goals, managing stress, and getting things done are at the very heart of a good quality of life.

I recently addressed a conference of professional organizers from all over the world. Can you imagine a conference of 1,000 extremely well-organized people *in one hotel?!* It must have been a nightmare for the hotel personnel. "Hello, front desk. Yes, this is Ms. Anal in Room 501. I'm attending the conference of professional organizers. I was wondering why the soap dish is on the left side of the sink rather than the right side?" Click. "Hello? Hello? Front desk?"

We organizers can dedicate entire workshops to the issue of filing categorically or hierarchically. But before you write us off as obsessive-compulsives who probably color-code our children, I want you to know that some very important knowledge that directly affects your quality of life came out of that conference.

My address to my colleagues, entitled "Getting Organized in the Era of Endless," reported a seismic change in the history of getting organized. The Era of Endless, which is upon us, is a real game-changer for people like you who are trying to get organized...and for the professional organizers trying to help you. As a busy person you're bombarded from all directions with endless information. You feel it in places usually reserved for leisure, like parks and restaurants and ball fields that vibrate with invisible tethers to endless work. You feel it in the palpable frustration of losing your train-of-thought and the incompletion of a task-at-hand because of endless distractions and interruptions. Your closets and garages and homes and offices quake with a seemingly endless amount of stuff.

All this endlessness—endless information, endless work, endless interruption, and endless stuff—butts right up against the one thing that remains intractably finite—time. Time can seem to fly, we can bide our time, sometimes the time is ripe, other times it is golden. We might live on borrowed time, or be ahead of our time, or, for that matter, behind the times; but no matter how we describe our relation to time, *we cannot make more time.* Time can be more effectively used and more efficiently allocated, but what there is of it is all there is of it and there will be no more of it. We can (and do!) make more information, connections, work, things to do, distractions, interruptions, and stuff but time remains finite. It is *not* growing, expanding, or becoming in any way *more.* Time is seemingly undergoing the opposite of endless. It feels like it is shrinking relative to all this endlessness.

It is tempting to blame technology for the challenge of getting organized in the Era of Endless. And certainly, technology plays a role. The stores, the banks, and our wallets are open 24/7 so we can get more stuff by simply turning on our smartphone. Work that is no longer restrained by buildings and time zones and bosses and offices bleeds over into our non-work life. Devices bring the awesome reach of the Internet to our fingertips, pockets, and vehicles. We can connect via emails, text messages, voicemails, tweets, alerts, comments, links, posts, tags, digital photos, videos, blogs, feeds, and apps. The same devices and apps that bring us entertainment, news, what's new, creativity, and information bring us interruptions, distractions and temptations. Blaming technology doesn't get us any closer to how to get and stay organized in the Era of Endless. It is against the very nature of technology to wish it would slow down or go in reverse. No. It is up to us to adapt.

Recently, the Judith Kolberg Award was established by the Institute for Challenging Disorganization (ICD). I'm extremely honored. As a thought-leader in my industry I am not satisfied to merely give you insightful thinking about the Era of Endless and the challenges it poses for getting organized. I am, first and foremost, a professional organizer. My job is to give you practical organizing solutions appropriate to the Era of Endless so you can adapt to this unique era. But first, let's take a step back and see just how getting organized has reflected and encouraged, in Morgenstern's words "...who we are, what we want, and where we are going."

Part One of this book traces the light-hearted history of getting organized through the lives of prehistoric Mona and her descendants. It ends with Elly, a descendant on the brink of the Era of Endless. Part Two describes the Era of Endless and its unique organizing challenges through stories about Elly's family, particularly her daughter Lisa who is living headlong in the Era of Endless. Parts Three through Six contain practical strategies and solutions.

---

[1] National Association of Professional Organizers, Quick Poll, 2012
[2] FileHeads Professional Organizers research, *New York Daily News*, *Reader's Digest*, and *Women's World Magazine*, 1990-2010

ERA OF ENDLESS

PART ONE

A RIDICULOUSLY SHORT HISTORY OF GETTING ORGANIZED

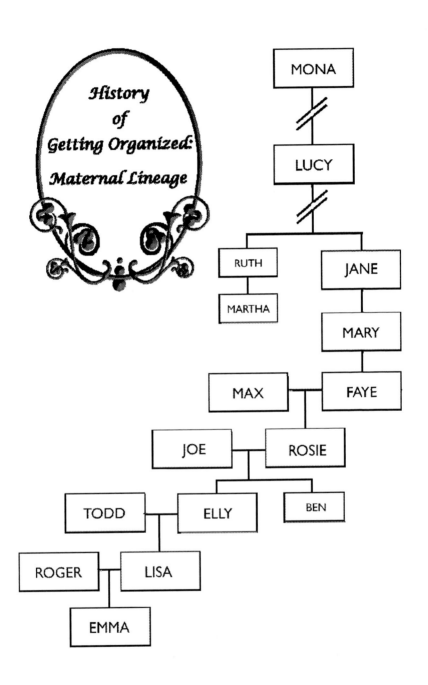

History of Getting Organized: Maternal Lineage

MONA

LUCY

RUTH — MARTHA

JANE

MARY

MAX — FAYE

JOE — ROSIE

TODD — ELLY — BEN

ROGER — LISA

EMMA

Getting Organized in the Era of Endless

A Ridiculously Short History of Getting Organized

Anthropologists tell us that earliest humans, like other primates, groomed one another. At some point, the evolutionary story goes, humans began to live in larger and larger groups and all this manual grooming began to take up more and more time. Early humans needed all their time for survival pursuits like hunting for food, roaming for food, and driving hostile animals away from their food.

Humans, it is thought, developed language partly as a way to *economize their time*. "Vocal grooming"—the use of words—was way more efficient than manual grooming for keeping the family and allies happy.[1] A few choice words could soothe and offer assurance, comfort, and the promise of protection instead of all that hair-parting, back-scratching, insect-removal grooming, however nice it must have felt.

Picture the first cave woman. Let's call her Mona. Mona has a large, extended family to groom, an infant to feed, hostile threats all around her, and several men fighting over her. It would have made any woman scream. Mona reached over to the emotional side of her big brain, integrated it with the verbal processing portion way over in the other hemisphere of her brain, focused her mind against all the distractions around her and transformed a simple sound into a meaningful word. Awesome.

No, "awesome" was not likely the first word. What's awesome is Mona's big-brain ability to economize time (yea, yea, language development is important, too). The economy of anything, whether it's money or space or time, is the effort to achieve the maximum effect for the minimum effort. The maximum effect Mona was trying to achieve was to cut down on all that manual grooming and instead use less effort with vocal grooming. Economizing her time, a fundamental organizing skill, also turned out to be a vital survival skill.

Mona economized time in other ways. She probably figured out how to maximize daylight and darkness. With her big brain she likely surmised from experience that spearing fish is dangerous and unproductive at night so getting it done in daylight gave her a survival edge.

Her cavemen clan surely took note that leading a raid on enemy tribes under the cover of darkness was an efficient use of night time. Self-preservation pretty much filled up Mona's entire day.

Economizing time *to jam non-survival activities into her 24 hour day* was not very important until hundreds and hundreds of years later when Mona's kin got a little agriculture going. Growing food rather than clubbing it produced a bit of down-time and engagement in activities beyond the crushing need to survive and procreate. It wasn't exactly *leisure time* in the sense we think of leisure today, but spending time in a diversity of activities provided advancement of the species, such as a little cave painting or maybe a walk to the shore to see the sunset.

How Mona chose to spend her time might have been severely limited but that does not mean Mona's day was devoid of decision-making. Probably she ate bark and beef and decided beef was a better choice because it agreed with her stomach, whereas bark contained more fiber than anyone ever needed. As the choices in her life multiplied, personal preferences may have emerged. "If I eat one more banana, I'm going to turn into an ape," Mona might complain. "I'd rather have a coconut." Decision-making in big brained humans is innate. We have an innate capacity for choosing and for deciding rather than merely reacting or letting the coconuts fall where they may. Organizationally speaking, making decisions expresses a certain mastery over our circumstances, adding yet another measure of quality to life.

Decision-making has another value. It is a great economizer of time. When we make decisions, we move a myriad of little tasks along to accomplishment, allowing us to make progress on more complex projects, keeping us on path to achieve goals. Decision-making today is as vital as spear-throwing was to Mona and her kin.

Cleanliness may be next to godliness, but orderliness is most assuredly next to humanliness. Refuse, garbage, and waste that breed itchiness, stench, and a certain squish between the toes when walking barefoot didn't seem to bother Mona much more than it did other animals. But lack of order probably got her goat. The word *order* is derived from the Latin *ordinem*: to give order to, to arrange. Orderliness was very likely another organizing survival skill. "What a mess!" Mona might have said. "My food is mixed in with these damn rocks and sticks. If I separate out the sticks from the foody things maybe the kids won't keep choking over dinner and we can get through a darn meal together. I'll sort out the little rocks and put them over there with the big rocks and maybe move the whole stack of rocks way over there so I don't keep tripping on them. Maybe I'll put all the sticks together so I can have them handy to stoke the fire, pull the bugs out of my ears, or whatever."

Did Mona sort and categorize? There is evidence from caves and other early dwellings that even the most primitive humans put like-things together and separated them from other like-things based on function. There were distinct areas for cooking and eating, tossing garbage, and even leisure activities like carving stones.

Could it be that the human inclination to orderliness and the ability to sort and categorize gave Mona's family and tribe an evolutionary edge? I'm not the first to suggest this. In the book, *A Perfect Mess: The Hidden Benefits of Disorder,* authors Eric Abrahamson and David H. Freeman observe that for cavemen:

> "...a preference for certain types of order must have conferred certain advantages in his fight for survival: a knack for categorizing mushrooms into poisonous and non-poisonous varieties, for keeping hunting grounds free of human signs that would tip off prey, for storing precious tools and hides in one corner of the cave to enable fast packing and swift flight in case of emergency..."

The authors go on to say that "We are literally born categorizers and for good reason: *there isn't enough time* when we encounter each new entity in the world to go through the process of carefully observing and analyzing it so that we can finally decide if we need to pet it, eat it, flee from it, or smile at it." Sorting and categorizing, it turns out, are also great ways to economize time. Child development research supports the inborn ability of humans to categorize. Even infants, as young as six months can associate pictures of Siamese kittens and Tabby kittens and other kinds of kittens into the category "kitty."

Putting things in reasonable access for ease of use is another basic organizing skill and this is what we often mean when we use the word *organize*. Chances are Mona figured out if she put a club right by the cave opening and another near where the baby slept, and if she put the kindling right near the firestones, her *stuff*, meager as it was, would be organized in support of her priorities: survival and reproduction. It would be literally at-hand. Ancient habitats reveal essential fluids, including water, wine, and olive oil, were contained in pottery, leather, and wooden vessels along with the inclined planes to move them around; but what brilliant Homo sapien figured out how to store things inside storage spaces? "I need closet space!" Mona would have railed. Clay cubbies and stone shelves lined prehistoric dwellings in Africa, the Middle East, and China. Organizing tools like the nook, cranny, sack, hook, and cubby rank right up there with the lever, wheel, pulley, inclined plane, and wedge. In fact, the word *organize* shares a root with the word for *tool*. And the Pyramids? One big closet.

The mega-organizing skills of economizing time and decision-making, along with other organizing skills like sorting, categorizing, containing stuff, and keeping things handy and accessible immensely improved Mona's quality of life. Even though meteors spooked Mona's food into extinction, humans survived. Organizing skills likely contributed to their evolutionary edge.

The Invention of Lists

Millenniums later, Mona's descendent invented the list, an innovation so profound many of today's humans feel they would become extinct without it. The notion of the list dates back to ancient China, not surprisingly because they also invented paper. The ancient Chinese made lots of lists and stowed them together in scrolls inside special cupboards. Most common were inventory lists of grains in storage, animals on the farm, trees in the kingdom, building supplies in storerooms, and wares loaded and unloaded onto ships. There were lists of people too: palace employees, males capable of bearing arms, and enemies of the Pharaoh, King, or Emperor, depending on the country. The Bible is replete with lists of animals on the ark, lists of ancestors, and lists of commandments and sins. The checklist likely evolved from the inventory list. "Noodles? Check. Fish? Check. Rice wine? Hey, who forgot the rice wine?" the narrative might have gone.

But the To-Do list is the true marker of human development. As crucial as the To-Do list is, there's no historical account of its inventor and no national holiday to mark the occasion of its birth. So let's assign one: Lucy, Mona's descendent.

Lucy had a big brain even for a human! She could write, and specified each task longwise on a piece of parchment or on a scroll. Lucy still used the sun and the moon, the stars and the tides, and the seasons to chart the passage of time. But most significantly, Lucy had faith in the future. She trusted that tomorrow would come and not only would she be an active participant in it, but also be able to control what happened, at least to some extent. She could do this by jotting down tasks that needed to be done *later*.

Tomorrow always came, though not everybody survived to see it. An occasional eclipse would shake everyone's faith about whether the sun would ever shine again, but a few hundred human sacrifices would set everything right. Slowly, a kind of involuntary shaping of the subconscious was taking place, a subliminal, rudimentary path towards planning based on future-sense. The organizing skill of planning and the tools that go with it, such as the To-Do list, calendar, and schedule, took their place in history.

"As an inherent force in nature and within human beings, planning assumes great significance. It may be the most effective force ... and among the most basic compulsions in man," writes Melville Branch, author of *The Planning Imperative in Human Behavior*. Lucy and her kin were compelled to plan because they could not help looking forward to tomorrow. Future-sense was becoming hard-wired into human beings.

We are not the only species with the capability of planning for the future. Santino is a chimpanzee who lives in a zoo in Stockholm, Sweden. Prior to human visitors entering the zoo each day, Santino develops a deceptive plan. He gathers stones and concrete projectiles to throw at zoo visitors. A 2010 study proves he plans for this future event by concealing the objects in hay and other places proving that forethought is not exclusively human. But Santino cannot compare with Lucy. Her forethought ability and faith in the future gave rise to the revolutionary planning instrument, the To-Do list. No longer were humans merely recording, tracking, accounting, or tallying items. The To-Do list represented tasks to do and actions to accomplish *in the future.*

Timekeeping

Not even the calendar can match the To-Do list's power. The Egyptian calendar is among the oldest in the world. Amenemhat, the great clerk to the Pharaohs, would use it to chart the phases of the moon and the passage of seasons. But the calendar is past-oriented. Jeremy Rifkin wrote in his timeless (ha!) book, *Time Wars: The Primary Conflict in Human History.* "The calendar's legitimacy rests on commemoration …of myths, ancient legends, heroic deeds of the gods…and the cyclical fluctuations of astronomical and environmental phenomena." In short, things of the past that tend to repeat were recorded on a calendar.

As major religions arose, calendars become even more significant. Each group began their calendar at a kind of ground zero date for the birth of their religion. Thus the Gregorian calendar begins with the birth of Christ, the Jewish calendar with the date of creation, and the Muslim calendar with the flight of Muhammad from Mecca. Holy days, rites of passage, saints' birthdays, and other recurring religious occasions forged even more religious cohesion.

By the Middle Ages, quality of life was improving unless you were a debtor, a Jew, or had the Black Plague. Increasingly, people needed to know what time it was, not just in that "is-it-time-to-plant-the-corn?" kind of way, but also because daily life was getting more complex. Peasants and farmers could still divide their day by the passage of the sun, but priests and monks, especially Benedictine monks who played an active role in village life during the Middle Ages, were responsible for performing daily rituals and communal prayer. This was no small deed. Entire villages had to come together to pray at various times of

Getting Organized in the Era of Endless

the day and the monks themselves needed to gather for prayer seven times a day between midnight and lights-out at 9 PM.

Lucy's To-Do list was a beautiful thing but sixth century Benedictine monks would trump it by inventing the schedule. Much of the scheduling of village and pastoral life was accompanied by bell ringing. Gradually, the schedule seeped out of the monastery and into secular society. The rising merchant class lent itself well to scheduling. There were schedules for ship departures and arrivals, schedules of loading times, schedules for the shifts of labor, schedules for payments due, and schedules for hanging people who missed that deadline.

Life synchronized to bells soon translated nicely into clock-time. Monastic communities kept track of the time by various means including water clocks, sundials, astrolabes, and well-trained body clocks from years of practice. The Great Race to mechanize timekeeping was on. Finally, experiments with gearing systems and weights led to the invention of the first truly mechanical clock late in the thirteenth century. Just fifty years later, most towns boasted a clock in the town square to regiment church services, regulate working hours, and allow crafts-men to bill by the hour. Time was not yet money because the medieval economy was still 85% subsistence agriculture; but the historical connection between time and money was emerging.

The Rise of Information

Something else was also emerging in the complex European world of trade and commerce: an increase in information. Decisions needed to be made about what was necessary to know. Then that information needed to be sorted, categorized, and contained. Organizing information was not a new enterprise. Nobody organized information better than the Romans. The oldest encyclopedia, *Naturalis Historia*, was written in AD 77 **and still exists!** Pliny the Elder, its author, was a kind of Thomas Jefferson type of guy, an author, naturalist, philosopher, and naval and army commander of the early Roman Empire. While at sea or on land, he investigated natural and geographic phenomena. *Naturalis Historia* became a model for all encyclopedias to follow. In the east, the administrative aspects of the Chinese court with its sophisticated clerks, scrolls of laws, and recording of "all things Confucius" was light years ahead of any western version of information organization.

Between 1500 and 1700, European explorers took to the seas discovering many lands including the New World. The great civilizations of the Incas and Aztecs fell. The plus and minus signs (almost as important as the To-Do list!) took their place in society. Michelangelo and Leonardo da Vinci rose to fame.

There's nothing like war to bring societal order to its knees and during this period Europe had plenty of it. Lucy's descendant, Jane, had enough of the chaos and split for the New World to practice her religion without persecution and to farm the land unmolested by war or natural disasters. These were hard times. New England winters brought hardships of biblical proportion. Starvation and disease were rampant. Women were burned at the stake. But the colonists persevered. The Protestant work ethic tying salvation to hard work and frugality allowed them to hold on.

Events far worse confronted the non-white population of Native Americans and African slaves. The Plains Indians invented a collapsible tepee to break camp quickly so they could follow the buffalo and escape the White man.

In 1700 we find Jane living in Boston, the young nation's largest city. Boston was a vibrant city. Among its native sons is Ben Franklin, Mr. Efficiency himself. Franklin's printing press, way improved since the days of Gutenberg, generated written tracts of all kinds: political, religious, and educational. As written information expanded, word-of-mouth, the oldest form of information, diversified. Citizens could listen to traveling minstrels, debates on the soap box at the corner, and if they had more education and money, they could join educational societies and literary clubs.

For the first time, books were not just for religious or academic study but for personal entertainment, evidence of a rising literacy rate and an increase in leisure time. Jane read books and newspapers including Benjamin Harris' *Publick Occurrences Both Forreign and Domestick*, the first of many newspapers in the American colonies. (It published just one edition before being suppressed by a government not quite accustomed to colonists slandering the Crown.) Jane and her contemporaries craved information especially about politics. Britain and France, the dominant colonial powers, divided the colonies and imposed new taxes on the colonists, who had no representation in Parliament. In 1775 rebels in Massachusetts launched the Revolutionary War by clashing with British troops. A year later, the colonial delegates met in Philadelphia and declared their independence.

Meanwhile, Franklin scanned his office loaded with tracts and pamphlets, newspapers and business documents that now required organizing, and declared, "A place for everything and everything in its place." The origin of this expression might actually have its roots in the domestic scene. It first appeared in a story called *The Naughty Girl Won*, published by the Religious Tract Society, a Christian literature publisher in England. "Before, however, Lucy had been an hour in the house, she had contrived a place for everything and everything in its place."

Jane loved the poetry and depth of meaning of the Declaration of Independence but she admired even more the orderliness of the checks and balances of the Constitution with its three branches of government. She wondered if Mary, or any of her other daughters would ever be able to enjoy the right to vote, now limited to male, white property owners.

The United States Post Office, recently founded, delivered a letter to Jane. It was from her sister who lived in a town that would later be known as Chicago. The letter encouraged Jane to move out West to start a life away from the big city. Life definitely was getting more complicated in Boston and other large cities. If you added up all the minstrels, tracts, newspapers, mail, books, pamphlets, business documents, and couriered messages, there was still no danger that Jane would suffer from "information overload." Still, she kept the West in the back of her mind.

In the late 1700s, the majority of people worked on farms producing food but by the mid-1800s that had shifted. More and more people were working in trades, factories and mills and the owners and managers of those enterprises were very much attuned to (labor) time being money. "Remember that time is money," Franklin notes in his 1748 tract entitled *Advice to a Young Tradesman.*

Across the pond, John Letts launched his stationery business in London, England's center of commerce. Merchants and traders frequented his shop clamoring for diaries that enabled them to arrange transactions by date such as stock movements (livestock, that is) and sales of commercial goods. Letts ledgers and diaries not only recorded who owed how much to whom but also *when it was due.* (Letts is still in business, one of the oldest continuously operating companies in the Old or the New World.)

As England launched the Industrial Revolution, back in the States, the issue of slavery began to divide the nation. Jane's daughter, Mary became a Quaker involved in a network of safe houses and hideaways known as the Underground Railroad. Jane supported freeing the slaves but felt her daughter Mary was in danger. Recalling her sister's letter, Jane and her husband moved the family to Chicago right before the first shot was fired at Fort Sumter. The ensuing Civil War raged for four years. The Union with its larger population, stronger industrial base, and eagerness to reunite the nation, won the war in 1865.

Mary adjusted to life in the Midwest. Education was finally separated from religion and became universal. Melville Dewey, an educator, and like Franklin a master of American ingenuity and efficiency, even went to the extent of dropping the "excess" letters in his first name to become Melvil. Dewey founded the Library Bureau which sold high quality index cards and filing cabinets, establishing the standard dimensions for catalog cards. Mary found books in the public library guided by the Dewey Decimal System including Lyman Frank Baum's *The Wonderful Wizard of Oz*, which she read to her little girl, Faye. Mary ordered clothing and shoes from the Sears catalogue but today we regard catalogues as a nuisance. For hundreds of thousands of people on the frontiers, farms, and prairies of America, receiving their mail order catalogues was a much anticipated event.

Getting Organized in the Era of Endless

Timekeeping Redux

Quality of life at the dawn of America's Industrial Revolution improved so much that food production soared, the spread of childhood diseases lessened, and as a result the population exploded. Huge numbers of people needed to be absorbed into the economy. Mass production conducted in factories and mills driven by hydroelectric and steam power fit the bill. That infernal bell ringing of the medieval towns and clock-time honed over several hundred years enabled what historian Lewis Mumford called "the great synchronization," the beat of labor to the tempo of the assembly line. Mary's cousin, Martha, lived in Connecticut and worked on the assembly line in Eli Whitney's musket factory. Whitney's assembly line used standardized and interchangeable parts, an innovation that became the gold standard for economizing time until a man named Henry Ford raised the efficiency bar even higher.

In 1875, Alexander Graham Bell and Thomas Watson succeeded in carrying voice over telegraph lines by converting undulating vibrations into sound. Just ten years later, 150,000 people in the US owned telephones. In 1904, Max Weber wrote *The Protestant Ethic and the Spirit of Capitalism,* and though the country was no longer only Protestant, capitalism raised quality of life to new heights. Mary, now with a family and home of her own, installed a telephone at home. She worked as a secretary at the regional Bell Telephone company, rolling her boss's business papers into tight scrolls, tying them with cord, and sticking them into "pigeonholes" lining the walls. When Edwin Grenville Seibel invented wooden filing drawers, Mary reorganized the business documents. She inserted them into large envelopes which stood on end vertically inside the filing cabinets.

Years later, cheap hemp fiber available from Manila, Philippines, was used to create "Manila" file folders. Mary liked to think that Baum got the idea for the word "Oz" from a filing cabinet drawer labeled "O-Z." Near the end of his life Seibel was awarded a bronze plaque that read, "Business throughout the world has been helped by this idea and on it has founded an industry that provides employment for many men and women."

America was beginning to become a document-dense nation. Even in the home, people kept receipts in the event a bolt of fabric or other purchase needed returning. Personal letters tied with ribbon and stowed in roll-top desks, could easily be read and re-read. Diaries and ledger books of household expenses were common; baptismal papers were hidden in Bibles; life, health, and other insurance policies proliferated. Babies born in hospitals (a new occurrence) went home with birth certificates and banks issued passbooks. The federal income tax law was passed in 1913 forcing every family to keep better financial records.

But a family's most cherished document might be citizenship papers. America, the great melting pot, welcomed unprecedented numbers of immigrants to its shores. Mary's little girl, Faye played with the children in her Chicago neighborhood: German, Russian, Italian, and Hungarian who came by train from Ellis Island, New York. Between 1860 and 1920, foreign-born immigrants accounted for between 13% and 15% of the US population. Life in America for many immigrants began on the ships boldly boarded by families knowing little about what the future held but moved to unspeakable inspiration by the Statue of Liberty. Immigration officials boarded the ships and efficiently examined passengers for obvious diseases like cholera, measles, and smallpox. Those who passed muster were disinfected, vaccinated, and issued name tags and manifest numbers.

Armed with a 31-point questionnaire, the immigrants divulged, through a battery of interpreters, their age, sex, country of origin, and other vital information designed to identify and sort out criminals and the insane. Even watching the immigrants climbing up the stairway to the Registry Room was a way to categorize people. Doctors at the top of the stairway looked for signs of pulmonary and heart disease and marked with chalk the coats of those who needed further medical examination. Those not detained or returned to their home countries, received the coveted landing card (pinned to their clothes), exchanged their marks and shekels for US dollars, and were sent to the railroad office or ferry with a ticket and a boxed lunch. If there was an award for "Getting Organized" near the turn of the new century, it would surely go to the immigration officials at Ellis Island.

Mary's daughter, Faye, became the first in her family to attend college. She studied business and greatly admired the work of Italian economist, Vilfredo Pareto. Pareto observed that 80% of the land in Italy was owned by 20% of the population. The Pareto Principle, as it is known, holds up consistently in many areas of life. 80% of sales, for instance, is derived from just 20% of customers. Faye used this principle to guide her life, even looking for the 80/20 advantage in her wardrobe!

After graduation, she worked at the Ford Motor assembly plant in office management where she met her husband, Max. They married at the dawn of World War I. She was an adventurous woman who did not want mundane housekeeping to stop her from seeing the world. Home appliances such as the vacuum cleaner, electric iron, toaster, and refrigerator helped her economize time, maximizing a well-kept home with minimum effort. She and Max climbed into their Studebaker and took a road trip to Yellowstone National Park. Theodore Roosevelt, the Conservation President, created our national parks system in part to protect the parks, but also in anticipation that hard-working families would soon take to the road in their new automobiles in search of economical vacations.

Frederick Winslow Taylor, meanwhile, figured out how to squeeze every last bit of productivity out of Americans before they could pack their bags. Taylor's *Principles of Scientific Management* published in 1911, took getting organized to new heights. "Conservation of our national resources is only preliminary to the larger question of national efficiency, the great loss which the whole country is suffering through inefficiency in almost all of our daily acts," Taylor maintained. Faye was now a manager at the Ford Motor company. Her job was to study, measure, and record every element of every manual task performed by the workers in her department of the factory. She was an "efficiency expert" with a stopwatch and notebook charged with standardizing every movement of the factory workers to achieve maximize output.

Taylor was certain the fundamental principles of scientific management perfected on the factory floor were applicable to all kinds of settings including homes, farms, churches, and government. Indeed, many women believed that Taylorism could curtail the drudgery of time-consuming household maintenance and childcare. The American Home Economics Association was founded in 1909 based on scientific management principles. Magazines such as *The Ladies' Home Journal* began to offer articles about scientific management.

But Taylorism pushed efficiency too far. Maximizing effect and minimizing effort was a sound goal, but humans are not machines. The workers in Faye's factory objected to being treated like they were interchangeable parts and revolted against the dehumanizing nature of scientific management, the speeding up of tasks, and the reduction in take-home pay. Eventually their demands led to the rise of labor unions. Nonetheless, scientific management left a great legacy to the history of getting organized including documenting processes, improving the transfer of knowledge among workers, and the evolution of what became known as "best practices."

In 1914, vast armies faced each other across thousands of miles of trenches and fortifications in Europe. In 1916, US neutrality broke and we entered the war. A rapid ramp up of soldiers, weapons, ships, logistics, and supplies was necessary. A military-industrial complex of boards, offices, and administrations was formed to plan and mount a World War. Americans "Hooverized." They went wheatless on Wednesdays and meatless on Mondays, conserving food so that more was available to ship to the starving children of our European allies. American food exports tripled. President Wilson urged citizens to support the Red Cross. Civilians contributed to the war effort by making masks, staffing hospitals, giving blood, driving ambulances, and knit-ting woolen socks.

The period from World War I through the Roaring Twenties was an era marked by uunprecedented industrial growth, accelerated consumer demand, and significant cultural richness. Faye voted! Her west coast cousins attended the San Francisco 1915 World's Fair, a great place to see what the future holds. Cross-country calls were made every day of the Fair on Alexander Graham Bell's improved telephone. General Electric demonstrated indirect lighting. A small model of Henry Ford's assembly line turned out one car every 10 minutes for three hours every afternoon.

The Direct Marketing Association was established in 1917 to facilitate business-to-business postal communication. Unsolicited mail from commercial businesses was a new occurrence. Faye received one-cent post cards with printed advertisements from companies like General Electric that seemed perfectly timed to when her washing machine broke down and needed replacement.

Her work done at home, Faye might go to the picture show, a ballgame, or out dancing. Although it would not become the law of the land until 1938, many employers were beginning to observe the 40-hour week based on research that productivity actually declined after 40 hours. Leisure time was now official!

The good times rolled until they didn't. Although the 1920s appeared on the surface to be prosperous, income was unevenly distributed. The wealthy made large profits, but more and more Americans spent more than they earned, and farmers faced low prices and heavy debt.

The lingering effects of World War I caused economic problems in many countries, as Europe struggled to pay war debts and reparations. Stock prices fell and investors pulled out of the stock market. In 1929 it crashed. Little boys bought Lincoln Logs, Erector sets, and Tinker Toys but grown-up building projects came to halt. Businesses went belly up. Banks failed. Faye and everyone else she knew lost their jobs. They stopped buying things at the store which caused more businesses to fold, resulting in even more unemployment. 25% of the workforce was unemployed during much of the ten year period of The Great Depression. For the first time since the poverty-stricken days after the Civil War, scarcity ruled the day.

Waste Not Want Not

The Great Depression would significantly imprint the very foundation of our notion of getting organized. Just as the Protestant work ethic would discourage wasting time, the "waste-not-want-not" ethic of the Great Depression discouraged waste of goods. This expression originated in a 1772 letter written by John Wesley, founder of the Methodist Church. Observing economic conditions around him in England, he coined the phrase that meant if a person does not waste what they now have, they will not be in need of it later. Ben Franklin utilized the expression as well, but the Depression-era film, *Topper Takes a Trip,* that Faye watched with her daughter, Rosie, really brought the message home for Americans.

Thrift in all things turned a piece of rubber into a shoe sole and the day's garbage into someone's meal. Electric lights in the house were turned off. The American Plains turned into a Dust Bowl when unprecedented dust storms destroyed crops, eroded the soil, and starved many people who attempted to live on the desolate land. So deeply felt were the economizing practices of the Depression that the children of the children of the Depression (the Baby Boomers) would themselves, even in a time of prosperity, hesitate to divorce themselves from goods they no longer wanted or needed.

President Franklin Delano Roosevelt created programs, collectively known as the New Deal, to overcome the effects of the Great Depression. Government programs employed millions of people in housing, farming, highway construction, and bridge projects. Social-assistance measures like the Social Security Act and Medicare were implemented on the national level. But it was the massive spending for World War II that really brought the country out of the Great Depression.

The bombs began to fall in Europe and the news on radio, in magazines, and in newspapers captured the attention of the public. From now on, Americans would never be far from a news source. Staying informed would henceforth always be a part of staying organized. In 1941, the Japanese bombed Pearl Harbor. Rosie riveted. She planted her victory garden, bought war bonds, conserved gas, and rationed shoes, fats, and cans. She listened to the radio as Hitler moved halfway to his Final Solution to exterminate all of Europe's eleven million Jews. Scientists learned to split the atom, weaponize it, and bring the war to an end with the bombing of Nagasaki, Japan, in 1945.

Scientists also learned how DNA was organized. And there was plenty of DNA to study. Just one year after the end of the World War II, 3.8 million babies were born in the US, including Rosie's daughter, Elly, and her siblings. Rosie's family took full advantage of the newfound peace and prosperity of the post-war era. She married Joe, a veteran who became a high school teacher educated on the GI bill. They moved from the city to the burgeoning suburbs, bought a black and white television set and a car, and had a bunch of kids that were sent to public school. Rosie's and Joe's life was not ideal like *Leave It To Beaver,* but the routines of civilian life suited them. Joe and thousands of other GIs returned with soldier routines adapted for family life like daily morning and evening toothbrushing (which had been intermittent prior to then), shoe polishing, and tool organizing perhaps carried over from weapon maintenance.

Routines are a great economizer of time. Rosie served fish every Friday, she did the laundry on Wednesdays, the family ate spaghetti on Saturdays, and spring cleaning always began May 1st, regardless of the official start of the season. Advances in the chemistry of rubber prompted by military manufacturing inspired James Caldwell and his wife, Madeline, to invent a rubberized, colorful dustpan which launched a new company called Rubbermaid, later called Newell Rubbermaid.

The family car improved quality of life immensely. Getting to work, grandma's house, the doctor, and the post office were all easier. Rosie became very adept at organizing her time around a circle of errands that grew to include the gas station, bank, supermarket (a new phenomenon), convenience store, and fast-food restaurant. She learned to juggle several tasks at once. She divided her attention and became what today we would call a "multi-tasker." Motorola car radios had been a feature in cars since the 1930s, albeit with some caution. Automotive historian Michael Lamm says, "Opponents of car radios argued that they distracted drivers and caused accidents, that tuning them took a driver's attention away from the road, and that music could lull a driver to sleep." The Auto Club of New York polled its members and 56% feared the car radio was a "dangerous distraction." The public won out and car radios became standard. Rosie was really put to the test while listening to the car radio, driving to McDonalds, rolling down the car window, talking to her passengers, and eating in her car without having an accident. She passed the test magnificently.

As for the car, America outfitted it with larger trunks to hold bags of groceries for large growing families, automatic windows for drive-through lanes, and specially treated fabric to repel stains from spilled French fries and ketchup. Fifty years later, the car, with its transportation heart still intact, evolved into a mobile office, testing the very limits of the human brain's ability to divide attention.

Distraction and Interruption

Rosie learned, without even realizing it, that getting organized in the twentieth century required multitasking, accommodation of distraction, and tolerance of interruption. Television was the great instructor in these skills. It was television that truly introduced distraction into the house. Rosie, a seasoned cook, would burn the roast more than once because she was distracted by the Ed Sullivan Show. If Rosie was not careful, her teenage daughter, Elly, and the younger kids would be glued to TV and neglect their homework. Rosie's family coped by bringing TV dinners into the living room, but distraction (the dividing of attention from a task-at-hand to something else) began in earnest.

Television introduced another organizing element into the American family: tolerance of interruption. Commercials interrupted programming with advertisements. The first commercial broadcast on a tiny black and white TV was by the watch-maker Bulova, who paid nine dollars for the ad that aired right before a baseball game between the Brooklyn Dodgers and Philadelphia Phillies. The ten-second spot displayed a picture of a clock superimposed on a map of the United States, accompanied by the voice-over "America runs on Bulova time." No image could have captured the nation's character more precisely: the increasing need to manage one's time, devotion to television, love of baseball, *and*, significantly, tolerance of interruption.

Rosie was also getting the hang of *fast*. Her expectation for how quickly it should take to complete mundane tasks began to change. She used her electric blender more and her mixing bowl less. She expected her letters to reach relatives on the opposite coast within five days rather than ten. Jesse Owens may have made history at the Olympics, but Rosie's new vacuum did its job in record time. Eugene Polley invented the Flash-Matic remote control in 1955. It looked like a ray-gun and though it could not zap aliens from Mars, it gave Americans unprecedented power to interrupt TV viewing and flip from channel to channel. The word "instant" entered the popular lexicon when John Glenn orbited the Earth drinking an instant breakfast drink called *Tang.* In 1947, Percy Spencer invented the "radarange," the first microwave oven based on radar technology developed during World War II. Rosie bought one as soon as it became available in 1954. America's passionate love affair with *fast* had begun in earnest. Getting organized would forever include doing things efficiently *and quickly.*

Everywhere she turned it seemed that technological devices made it easier for Rosie to economize time by spending less time on the mundane so she could chose to do other things with her time. She invited the many ladies in her Levittown community to attend Tupperware parties in her home. She loved the little "burp" sound made by the seal of Tupperware storage containers. The money she earned from Tupperware was recorded neatly in her bankbook and though the amount was small, it gave her a sense of security. She could use it for an emergency, a purchase, or it could just sit there earning interest. Saved money gave Rosie options.

Time saved from using labor-saving devices did not exactly work the same way. Rosie couldn't put the time she saved in a bank. It had to be used up as she went along. She could have chosen to invest in leisure activities like Mahjong, but she preferred her Tupperware business and traveled more than once to their Jubilee Conventions. When her microwave occasionally melted her Tupperware, Rosie recycled. (Recycling was nothing new. Dust and ash from pre-industrial English chimneys was used to create brick mortar, a much cheaper alternative to purchasing mortar on the market.) Rosie recycled not out of scarcity or necessity but because waste was over-abundant in her home. She recycled cans, plastics, glass bottles, and newspapers. It became a lifetime habit that she passed along to her children.

In 1964, President Lyndon Baines Johnson declared the war on poverty, and America was well on its way to becoming what sociologists called the first "post-scarcity society" (if you didn't count the Deep South and Appalachia). By 1970, Americans were so well-off President Nixon gave a state of the union address that called upon Americans to put happiness and "peace with nature" before greater material wealth. Most Americans owned a television, a phone, and a car. The prosperity and technologies of the 1960s did not, however, bring what anyone would call "happiness" to the period. The streets of major cities were aflame with rage against racism. President Kennedy, Dr. Martin Luther King, and Senator Robert Kennedy were all gunned down. Elly, now a teenager, made a mental note that "life is short," but it was actually get-ting longer. The projected lifespan of females like Elly, born in 1953, would be over 70 years, with many living into their 80s.

On a summer's evening in 1969 astronauts landed on the moon and it was better than drugs, sex, or rock and roll. That fall Elly's older brother, Ben, was at the University of Wisconsin in 1970 on a football scholarship studying the new field of computer science when a bomb exploded in protest over the University's connections with the military during the Vietnam War. By the time the Vietnam War peace accords were signed in 1973, the women's rights movement and the gay movement had begun, taking inspiration from the civil rights movement and the anti-war movement.

Elly wanted to be an environmentalist and clean the air and the ocean, but her personal environment was a mess. She rarely cleaned her room, rejected materialism and wore her T-shirts and jeans to tatters. Rosie worried. She insisted Elly "recycle" her Barbie dolls by donating them to poor children. Barbie was "born" about the same time as Elly when Ruth Handler watched her daughter Barbara playing with paper dolls. She noticed Barbara enjoyed giving them adult roles, instead of the usual representation of dolls as infants. Ruth suggested the idea of an adult-figured doll to her husband, a co-founder of Mattel. He was unenthusiastic about the idea. Ruth brought an adult-figured female doll home from Europe who "...knew what she wanted and was not above using men to get it."

Getting Organized in the Era of Endless

Barbie's femininity rather than her feminism would haunt her as the Feminist Movement took hold. But Barbie enabled over a billion girls to play out their fantasies whether it was to merely marry Ken or to be independently rich and glamorous. Elly's laziness was formidable and Rosie ended up packing her Barbies into Tupperware storage containers and stowing them in the basement where they stayed until Elly sold them on eBay after Rosie's death.

Electronic Information

Too bad there was no eBay in 1971. If Elly wanted to go to college, she'd have to get a job to help pay for it. That same year, a professor at the University of Illinois created the first electronic document by typing the *Declaration of Independence* into a mainframe computer. Not long afterwards, the floppy disc was invented and computers became an integral part of ordinary business. Elly cleaned up her act a little bit and got a job as a word processor. She became proficient at word processing and memorizing documents to a floppy disc. Elly printed documents because that was how they were passed around and a hard-copy version was needed for filing.

As the memory capacity of hard drives and external floppy discs increased, something interesting began to happen to the activity of organizing information. Technology and durable storage allowed Elly to create the document electronically and share the information by passing the floppy disc around. Elly revered her Post-it notes, a simple but incredibly useful invention of Dr. Spencer Silver, a chemist with 3M.

Organizing information shifted from culling information to capturing, indexing, and electronically filing the rapid expansion of information. In the 1970s, the Internet was utilized almost exclusively by the military and academia, but when this technology was loosed into the mainstream of American life in the 1980s, knowing-by-exclusion shifted to knowing-by-inclusion.[2]

In the next generation, information expanded exponentially and networked knowledge increased so much that one of the most significant organizing challenges would be how to organize information itself.

The Rise of Stuff

Elly graduated from college, went on to graduate school, and married Todd, but did not become an environmentalist. She became a psychologist. In the 1980s she eschewed corporate life and went into private practice, setting up her office at a business park close to home. During her peak working years, it was not unusual for Elly and her cohorts to regularly work 60 hours a work week. She and Todd rarely took vacations. But it paid off. Baby Boomers grew the gross domestic product by an astounding 78%. Elly and Todd purchased a home in a nice neighborhood and proceeded to accumulate many possessions largely because they were entitled to. "...Life, liberty and the pursuit of happiness" were rights written in the Declaration of Independence.

Elly's childhood home in Levittown occupied only 800 square footage; 1100 with the attic finished. Her parents, grandmother, and all four children lived there very comfortably. Elly's home was 1200 square feet and over the next 30 years Boomers would live in homes in excess of 1700 square feet even though the average family was smaller and smaller. Closet renovations increased like gangbusters and consumers in the 50+ age bracket typically spent $1,000 to $2,500 for non-bedroom closet make-overs.[3]

What was all the stuff in Elly's home? Furniture, home décor, linens, clothing, and housewares. Not wanting to work themselves entirely to death, Elly and Todd also accumulated La-Z-Boy recliners, deck furniture, VCRs, TVs, audio cassette players, cameras, home exercise equipment, camping equipment, and sporting paraphernalia. Each figurine, framed picture, and room accessory (what professional organizers call "ambience clutter") represents just a little bit more than is necessary, a little bit extra, a little bit of luxury—all rewards for working long and hard.

Making do with things because they were in limited supply, too expensive to replace, or difficult to come by may have started in the Depression but the ethic persisted in many post-World War II families. The dictum "use it up, make it last, wear it out" lived side by side with newfound prosperity. Todd and Elly fell into a cozy relationship with

Getting Organized in the Era of Endless

their clutter as if it were a fond uncle with somewhat unsavory habits overstaying a visit.

One cold sleeting day Todd parked his car at the curb because the garage was too full for their second car, darted for the door with his raincoat over his head, slipped, and fell. Talk about a wake-up call. The very next day, Elly journeyed to the garage, a room not quite indoors or outdoors, to assess the stuff and figure out how to get rid of it. Stuff is a word so ambiguous it would be almost meaningless if not for the fact that everybody instantly understands exactly what it means. The very sound of it implies "too much." From the 1970s forward, getting organized would include organizing stuff as a major component.

Cartons of newspapers and magazines were fermenting on the floor, a set of clunky golf clubs from Todd's first (and last) foray onto the course occupied a corner, and tennis rackets graduating from heavy wood to titanium hung on the wall. The sight of Coleman coolers made Elly's memory drift to the beach, the warm sun in her eyes as she lifts a beer to her lips and munches on a sandwich. The smell of paint and mildew brings her back to the present. The image of the sun above is replaced with folding chairs hitched to the ceiling. Todd's broken bicycle is manacled to the wall like a medieval criminal. There are tools, shovels, a lawn mower, rope, and a sack of screws bought in bulk weighing in at 80 pounds; a huge TV, cheap radio, dot matrix printer, collapsible clothes line, and Venetian blinds. Unusable but not yet waste, they linger, gradually losing their substance and meaning. The sheer durability of Elly's stuff posed organizing challenges for her. These were not disposables easily transported to the trash or recycling.

She tries and fails to summon up enough enthusiasm to plan the garage decluttering. Just the thought of it overwhelms her. She turns and walks out of the garage through the door that connects to the kitchen. In her large, well-organized, clean, brightly lit kitchen she decides to call in a professional to do the job.

"Getting organized" had long been a best-selling sector of the self-help segment of book publishing[4] and national seminar companies. For the first time, overwhelmed residential homeowners and stressed corporate managers began to engage professional help to get organized. The emerging field of professional organizing matched with the already well-rooted home organizing product and storage industry giants, like Tupperware and Rubbermaid, gave people like Elly a leg up on their organizing problems. The Container Store expands, and Office Depot opens. The National Association of Professional Organizers is born in 1986 in Los Angeles with the recognition that the Ellys and Todds of the world would pay for help to get organized.

Material comfort did not bring satisfaction and quality of life to everyone. The divorce rate soared, single parenthood was on the rise, and fear of success supplanted fear of failure for many Boomers. When Elly was not working at her job, she was working on improving herself. "There is no shortage of demand for products and programs that allowed Americans, especially affluent female Baby Boomers, to make more money, lose weight, improve their relationships and business skills, cope with stress, or obtain a quick dose of motivation," Market-data Enterprises analysts observed. Elly's self-help audio cassettes, video tapes, binders, books, and newsletters were part of a self-improvement industry that raked in almost $3 billion a year during the 1970s and 80s.

Devices & De-acquisition

On the corporate front, Todd experienced formidable organizing challenges. He sold medical supplies (intravenous tubing, surgical masks, and the like) for an enormous multi-national corporation. Todd is a knowledge worker, someone who creates value by applying ideas to his work. Mostly, he sat in front of a desktop computer; this was not his father's vacuum cleaner salesman days.

He is judged by his output, or productivity, which is measured by how many medical supplies he sells and by how well he improves the selling process itself, not by the industrial-age standard of hourly work and overtime dedication. Gone are the days of factory, mill or office work with strict, pre-defined processes and outcomes.

How Todd spends his time, as long as it produces medical equipment sales or improves the sales process, is largely up to him. He could choose to do a bunch of small tasks or take a bite out of one of the many projects on his desk. The contrast between the office worker of the 1970s and the one of the new millennium was significant in a very important respect. Todd could still finish what he started. It was more challenging, for sure, but it could be done.

> "The office worker of the 1970s had numerous responsebilities and tools to manage, including multiple telephones that had to be answered when they rang because there was no voicemail. Still, it was a relatively disconnected world, and the array of competing tasks was much smaller than it is today. So it was easier to choose one and stay with it, while others waited quietly in the background. Today, thanks to our screens, as we work we're constantly contending with far more tasks than our minds can handle..." [5]

Priorities, once clear by virtue of easily recognized importance or time-oriented urgency, began to compete. Tasks of high importance on somebody else's critical path competed with tasks that directly increased bottom line profits; and those might compete with tasks suddenly required to beat the competition to market. There was always new software to learn and only a short arc on the learning curve in which to do it.

And now there was electronic mail to contend with. At first Todd welcomed email. It cut down on the interruption of people dropping unannounced into his office. It lowered the number of phone calls he received. But soon email upped the ante on response time. A prospective client who requested a proposal by mail could expect it in a week. A response to an email request for a proposal shortened it to three days. With all the lip service paid to knowledge work, judged by value and productivity rather than clock-time devotion, Todd noticed everyone was still working ridiculously long hours. Time itself seemed to be changing.

In the 1980s, US corporations, like the one Todd worked for, suffered from intense foreign competition and slowing domestic market growth. They searched for ways to increase productivity and efficiency. In addition to laying-off millions of middle managers, US corporations turned to consultants to get more out of the remaining employees. Todd's company sent him to the Franklin Institute.

Hyrum W. Smith, a 37-year-old graduate of Brigham Young University, started a business in his basement creating and marketing business courses and management seminars. Inspired by Benjamin Franklin's ideas about human values and quality of life, he called the company the Franklin Institute, Inc. Smith interpreted Franklin's philosophy to mean that peoples' happiness and inner peace do not come from owning things, but from identifying what is important to them and then making their lives conform to those goals. Smith attributed his company's success to Franklin's principles.

Stephen Covey embodied this principle in his 1989 publication, *The 7 Habits of Highly Successful People*, which has sold more than 10 million copies as of the printing of this book. Unlike time management books that preceded it with their emphasis on clock-driven efficiencies of the industrial age, Covey's self-help books connected getting organized to larger purposes, missions, goals and values.

Todd's problem was not the mismanagement of time, but the misalignment of his life with his values. This idea sounded to him a little like the self-help books Elly was reading at home. And in a way, Todd was correct. Covey's connection of use of time to life values promised overall self-improvement. Todd attended the Covey seminar and was provided with the Day Planner, a large, three-ring binder with paper planning aids, monthly and annual calendars, and various personal management aids, each requiring yearly refills. He clarified his goals, wrote his personal mission, and aligned his work with his values. He listened to instructional cassette tapes at home, compact discs in his car, and Bruce Springsteen's *Born In The USA* at home.

Todd crisscrossed the country selling medical supplies. Users of the Franklin time management systems were on the move, in planes, airports, on trains, and traveling between offices. Franklin responded with the Pocket Planner that fit in a suit coat pocket or small purse. To appeal to the increase of women in the managerial, executive, and boardrooms of corporate America, the company brought out a line of decorative filler pages and covers for its planners. The Day Planner was the centerpiece of an empire of seminars, training institutes, retail stores, products, and consulting services.

Critics maintained that using the bulky binders often consumed more time than they actually saved. The Franklin Institute revenue, however, told a different story. Even during the deep economic recession of the late 1980s and early 1990s, profits soared. The company changed its name to Franklin Quest reflecting acquisition of training and consulting companies and changed its name again to Franklin Covey when it merged with the Covey Leadership Center.

In the early 1990s, Todd replaced his Pocket Planner with a personal digital assistant (PDA). More and more, devices began to proliferate in Elly's and Todd's lives. There was the computer at work, the two desktop computers at home, and now the PDA. Email, while not a device, jumped the corporate fence and they were able to communicate with each other from home to office. Elly even had a phone in her car! It was the size of Todd's shoe and reminded him of the TV show *Get Smart* where the bumbling detective speaks into his shoe phone. They embraced all the technologies of the day, though Elly sometimes longed for paper and pen. Perhaps she suffers from "embodied interaction," a theory that posits that three-dimensional tools, like pad and paper and pens and pencils, are easier on the brain. "Paper's tangibility allows the hands and fingers to take over much of the navigational burden, freeing the brain to think. When we read and write on the screen, we expend a great deal of energy just navigating."[6]

Whatever the reason for Elly's nostalgia, there's no going backwards. Technological devices that maximize effect and minimize effort are so integrated into everyday life, that getting organized includes how to actually make the most of them without getting overwhelmed by the very tools meant to help us.

On their fiftieth birthdays, Elly and Todd joined a veritable army of Baby Boomers who plan to downsize by getting rid of stuff they no longer need or want and that their grown children have made plain they do not want either. "The hearse doesn't have a trailer hitch," observes Julie Hall, author of *The Boomer's Burden: Dealing With Your Parent's Lifetime Accumulation of Stuff.* The decision to downsize is thrown into high-gear when Todd squirrels his way into the attic looking for his old *Star Wars* video cassettes, "Man Lands On the Moon!" headlined newspapers, and Michael Jackson albums hoping they might be worth something like the stuff on *Antiques Roadshow.* Deftly he avoids asbestos-laden insulation, steps around boards with protruding nails, and holds back nausea at the sight of tiny mice skeletons in long-ago planted traps. As he ventures deeper and deeper into the recesses of the dark attic, the space becomes more and more narrow. Todd somehow manages to get wedged between the attic floor and the sharply pitched roof rafters. He is stuck. Elly has to call the fire department to free him. That does it. Todd and Elly agree to move to a smaller home with less stuff.

The move to a smaller home uses every organizing skill evolved by the human species over centuries, plus every innate skill in neurology, heredity, and DNA. Todd and Elly economize time by hiring Susan, a professional organizer. The organizing industry has sophisticated greatly from the days of a simple garage project a decade ago. Susan has a battery of new ways to get rid of old stuff: eBay, Craigslist, online auctions, and websites such as www.Freecycle.com, along with old stand-bys of charitable donations, consignment, recycling, yard sales, and hand-me-downs to relatives.

Susan has gone through an education and certification program. Elly and Todd benefit from her knowledge of project planning, change management, stress reduction, the latest in space optimization, time management, and clutter reduction. Together they plan and schedule the operation. They sort, categorize, and organize until everything is packed, unpacked, and made accessible with ease.

For the stuff they still cannot quite part with, Todd and Elly invoke their version of the ancient skill of containing; they rent a self-storage unit. Self-storage users traditionally rent temporarily for short periods during life changing events like a divorce or relocation. Unemployment might cause a person to seek work elsewhere and store their stuff until they resettle. But Todd is an entirely new kind of renter. "These new renters seem compelled to keep trading up, from a cozy personal closet say, to a garage-like room, and then to a second unit or even a third unit," notes Michael T. Scanlon, Jr. President of the Self Storage Association. Indeed, the number of US households renting storage units is fast approaching 10 million as Boomers hit their 60th birthdays. Self storage grows 740% since the 1980s to be the fastest-growing sector of the US commercial real estate industry.[7]

The lobby of Todd's self-storage facility, called Stuff is Us, is set up like the registration desk at a fancy hotel with two smiling employees in matching monogrammed knit shirts. The air-conditioning is pleasant and there are several lounge chairs, designer end tables, and current issues of *Real Simple* magazine. A huge high-definition plasma TV hangs on the wall turned to the home improvement channel. There's free coffee, free Wi-Fi, free one-day usage of a truck, and free first month's rent. Todd's storage unit, however, is costing him dearly. A 50 square foot unit can cost $95 for a month in most cities. For a year of storage, that's $1,140.

Here's the thing though. Unlike past renters, Todd is not storing collectibles, antiques, high-end furniture or business inventory. The entire content of his self-storage unit is worth about $600. Why is he storing it? "Because it's still good." Waste-not-want-not strikes again!

---

[1] R.I.M Dunbar, "Coevolution of Neocortical Size, Group Size and Language in Humans," *Behavioral & Brain Science*, 1993

[2] David Weinberger, *Too Big to Know: Rethinking Knowledge now that the Facts Aren't the Facts, experts are Everywhere, and the Smartest Person in the Room is the Room*, pg. 13

[3] *Closet Magazine* and Closetmaid surveys

[4] *Book Market Magazine*, 1980 - 1990

[5] William Powers, *Hamlet's Blackberry: A Practical Philosophy for Building a Good Life in the Digital Age*, pg. 59

[6] *Hamlet's Blackberry*, pg. 153

[7] Self Storage Association statistics, 2004-2007

ERA OF ENDLESS

PART TWO

THE ERA OF ENDLESS

THE ERA OF ENDLESS

Getting organized has played an important role throughout the ages in improving quality of life. Getting organized may have even given the earliest humans a survival edge. Every era has its organizing challenges. In Part One, we saw how organizing skills were developed as civilization became more sophisticated.

Lisa is living in a unique era, the Era of Endless and we begin her story in 2012. Lisa's challenges include infinite information, incessant interruptions, constant distractions, unbounded stuff, and unending work. But one thing has remained constant stretching all the way back to prehistoric Mona: Lisa has the very same twenty-four-hour day in which to live her life—no more, no less. So while information, interruption, work, distraction, and stuff grow, time remains intractably the same.

No wonder Lisa feels that getting organized is overwhelming. Let's take a closer look at the organizing challenges of the Era of Endless through a few short anecdotes about Lisa and her family. We'll discover how the Era of Endless requires not only an update to some traditional skills but also the introduction of new organizing skills.

Endless Information

Lisa is a first-year professor at a local community college, married with a young daughter. Her iPhone wakes her body and ever so slowly her mind wakes, too. Still in a bit of a fog because she rarely gets adequate sleep, Lisa follows her morning routine. (Thank goodness for routines. If she had to actually think, mornings would be even more difficult.) A motion detector on the stairs picks up her movements and turns on the lights. She mechanically walks the iPhone over to its charging station, clicks on the laptop, and stumbles over to the Keurig which is already dispensing coffee (a true miracle).

The house, already awake with tiny red and green lights glowing on various devices, is charming in its own techie way. Thirty-three emails have downloaded from Lisa's multiple email accounts just as the coffee is finished brewing. The digital printer has sent an email to tell her that it, too, needs breakfast—more paper. She can identify all the sounds emitted from her iPhone: it rings for calls, bings for texts, and chirps for tweets.

She kisses her husband Roger good-bye and hugs and cuddles six year old Emma. Roger will drop her off at elementary school on his way to work. Mixed in with the whirl of finding keys and missing shoes, and the clatter of breakfast are several verbal messages: "Mom, I need construction paper" and "Honey, don't forget to get the oil changed." Pushing the fragile scratch pad memory of her brain to its limits, Lisa assembles a mental To-Do list: buy coffee, printer paper, and construction paper. Change oil. This requires great concentration, but the biggest challenge is remembering to transfer her mental list into her iPhone task list. She thinks she might be better off just jotting the little list down but it seems she can never marry a pen and pad together at the same time.

Lisa's emails inform, solicit, recruit, entertain, alert, and query and she reacts in-kind by reading, responding, deleting, sharing, downloading, and printing. Links to websites, documents, and audio and video clips send Lisa out into a vast expanse of even more information. Of course, it is not always information in the strict sense of "informing." Much of where Lisa ends up on the Internet is the kind of information that keeps her abreast of what's new, whether she intentionally seeks it or involuntarily bumps into it. Aware of her attraction to "what's new" Lisa resists the temptation to log-in to Facebook knowing she will surely be late for work if she does.

Tangible paper has not yet disappeared from Lisa's life. The mail slot in her front door clangs with a noise like an old fashioned buoy bell as the envelopes delivered by the mailman hit the floor with a nostalgic plop. She has a little plaque on her cluttered desk quoting Einstein, "If a cluttered desk is a sign of a cluttered mind, of what, then, is an empty desk?" Since she gets most of her information online, she doesn't read a newspaper and her magazine stacks have shrunk because she no longer subscribes. But in their place, an equally abundant quantity of born-digital emails and electronic documents unavoidably require birth from the womb of the computer to the midwife of the printer. Lisa is highly suspicious of her snail mail which, though the paperless office was promised forty years ago, seems to be more abundant than ever. Credit card solicitations alone probably account for a good portion of the forty-one pounds of snail mail she receives each year.

On her hard drive, Lisa's feels "...the weight of all that weightless digital stuff," as *Hamlet's Blackberry* author William Powers describes it. Her computer desktop is pock-marked with so many icons, they have lost their individuality and now appear to her as something more like a chickenpox breakout than the signposts to information they once were. Her Favorites, Bookmarks, and RSS feeds are so numerous there is nothing special about them anymore. Lisa has popped the roof off her computer and headed for the cloud to store it all.

The Cloud. Whenever Lisa's mom, Elly, hears the term she imagines herself in a tent in the woods, breathing in the fresh air, and beholding, not a sky of endless stars, but a sky of endless binary bits of alphabet soup. Elly is certain The Cloud is a metaphor for endless information.

But the issue of endless information is more than just quantity. Elly can't quite put her finger on it, but it seems her daughter Lisa, a totally digital native, does not suffer from information overload. In fact, she seems anxious to acquire more information and more connections to people, events, and what's new. Elly cannot recall the last time Lisa, who was always outdoorsy as a kid, was among the real clouds. Elly worries about Lisa. But then again when it comes to being organized, Elly was not exactly the best role model for Lisa. Throughout their childhood, Elly's children were constantly pushing mail, coupons, newspapers, magazines, toys, and paper clutter aside on the lovely, Thanksgiving-infused dining room table to make way for a meal or homework.

Lisa prints out a Groupon coupon for an oil change, packs up her laptop, and heads for the community college where she teaches. Perhaps it is because she's in education, teaching the leaders of tomorrow, that Lisa feels compelled to have the most cutting-edge information available for her students. Try as she may, the edge seems in need of endless sharpening. The task of preparing a syllabus for next semester's class is an exercise in endless information. It has no bottom and no stopping point, unless you count sheer exhaustion or brick-hard deadlines. Lisa reviews academic journal articles, reads e-books, listens to podcasts, watches YouTube videos, and researches dozens of blogs and websites. She is so afraid she'll miss something vital to her students' education that she literally does not know when she is done.

When Elly was in college, traditional knowledge was bound by the hours the library was open, the limits of paper, the body of knowledge that existed on a topic, and the capacity of filing cabinets. But the Internet has no body and it can be scaled indefinitely. In the book, *Too Big to Know*, author David Weinberger points out that,

> "The pursuit of knowledge is one of the most profound of human goals. In an effort to manage what our brains cannot, we filter, winnow, and otherwise reduce information. Knowledge has been about reducing what we need to know...Rather than knowing-by-reducing to what fits in a library or a scientific journal, we are now knowing-by-including every draft of every idea in vast, loosely connected webs."[1]

This pursuit of knowledge-by-addition rather than reduction is unique to the Era of Endless.

Lisa's husband, Roger, and her mom notice how stressed Lisa can become in her fear of missing out on just that one more bit of information critical to her student's education. She rushes about more, is less attentive to Emma, and worries so much it affects her sleep. Recently, this syndrome was given a name, FOMO, or "fear of missing out."[2]

But there's another dynamic at play besides fear. Lisa is turned on by the search. She becomes driven to let one Google search lead to the next and stays glued to the screen in pursuit of the next nugget of information. It reminds Roger of when Elly, his mother-in-law, goes to Las Vegas. Winning a few quarters exhilarates her so much she gambles many times that amount just for the thrill. Similarly, Elly finds information thrilling.

It may be brain-based, this tendency to pursue endless information. Dopamine is a neurological chemical released in the brain when new things are learned, such as when a person does an Internet search.

It is the same chemical released when a person gambles, and when people take cocaine.[3] Another theory of information turn-on is that searching for one more bit of undiscovered information holds outsized significance to Lisa psychologically.[4] She keeps going because she thinks the yet-to-be-found information may be the best. Along the informational road, Lisa encounters serendipitous information, information she didn't even know she wanted or needed. Serendipitous information, though accidental or incidental to her main goal, stimulates her and gives enough "ah ha" moments to keep her engaged even longer in the pursuit of endless information.

And there is yet one more reason why Lisa falls prey to endless information. It is called, "the great unnailing." Facts, once the great end to informational pursuits, are no longer doing their job. Facts used to be stopping points that led back to unilateral experts and singular sources of authority. They were the final resort of disagreements, problems, and questions.

In the Era of Endless,

> "...facts lose their ability to nail down conclusions because there are always other facts that support other interpretations. We are living in the messy transition between expertise spoken in a single voice to networked expertise, from contained and knowable to linked and unmasterable. On the Internet, hyperlinks are less nails than invitations to source material, elaborations, contradictions, and opinion. They lead the reader out of the article, acknowledging that thinking is...unfinished, incomplete."[5]

Endless. Unfinished. Incomplete. These are concepts that don't jive well with our historical understanding of organizing information. It has always been a neatly, buttoned-up kind of activity expressed in encyclopedias, libraries, catalog cards, and such. For every fact Lisa finds there is a counter-fact. Lisa never knows when she is done, when enough is enough, or when she has come to a conclusion, or at least covered all the arguments. Because information is now endless, Lisa will have to learn a new organizing skill. She'll have to learn how to stop, or at least recognize stopping points.

During a special designated part of her class lectures, Lisa permits her students to tweet her. Professors of the past would no doubt be horrified at the intrusion of texts and tweets into the classroom. But in the Era of Endless, intrusions once considered interruptive, are evolving. Lisa likes the instant feedback and the immediate opportunity to correct an error or clarify a point. And she has found that students who might not participate otherwise, find the informality and anonymity of the texts and tweets an easy way to raise questions and interact in the classroom.

After teaching her classes for the day, Lisa heads out to run errands. Her GPS, vocal directions and an app indicating where the best prices are, direct her to the nearest office supply store and she buys printer paper and construction paper, then gets the oil changed. She tries in vain to remember the other items on her mental To-Do list. Receipts, little bits of information of nebulous value, begin to populate her purse, recording her purchases and ATM transactions. Maybe a cup of coffee will help her remember what she has forgotten. The cashier scans her Panera card which automatically generates four emails: an e-coupon for a free bagel, instructions on how to sign up for frequent shopper instant savings, a reminder for how to reset her password, and an invitation to sign up others for high-caloric rewards.

"Would you like a receipt?" Lisa is asked for the first time ever. She freezes. Receipts have always been part of the transaction. Entertaining the proposition that she doesn't *have* to take a receipt is a paradigm change for her. Lisa saves receipts in the hope of reconciling them to her credit card statement, with a deep longing to reconstruct her discretionary spending and get it under control. A paper receipt keeps her in touch, literally, with these intentions. The world's oldest piece of writing is a 5,000 year old receipt for clothing sent by boat from ancient Mesopotamia to what is now Bahrain, according to Dr. Irving Finkel, curator of the Middle East Department at the British Museum. No wonder they are hard to give up.

"Do you want your receipt?" the cashier asks again. Lisa can't cope with the intangibility of that, at least not right this minute. She compromises and permits the receipt to be emailed to her.

In all, Lisa will encounter over two hundred information artifacts in her environment by lunch time.[6] They include emails, texts, tweets, and calls.

What's New

Historically, information has served multiple purposes, most predominantly to:

- inform
- answer a question
- solve a problem
- make a point
- satisfy a curiosity, and
- bring us up-to-date.

Staying up-to-date on current events and the news of the day has a long and proud history in Lisa's family tree. Her grandparents read newspapers and listened to the radio religiously. Her parents tuned in to TV news at 6:00 and 11:00 every night, read a daily and a weekend newspaper, and gleaned *Life Magazine* and *Newsweek*.

In the Era of Endless, news choices have multiplied. Newspapers and news magazines are on the decline, but they are replaced many times over with online media, blogs, 24/7 Internet radio, Internet TV, cable and network TV, news feeds, and news apps. The challenge for Lisa is managing a diverse, well-rounded news stream without getting saturated.

Another type of information has arisen to prominence: **what's new**, not to be confused with news. What's new arrives through many conduits including emails, texts, voicemails, tweets, alerts, comments, links, tags, posts, apps, feeds, filters, documents, photos, videos, movies, web pages, music, audio files, computer games, downloads, Instagrams, likes, friends, and fans (and no doubt other conduits born since the writing of this book). What's new can arrive in the middle of a funeral service on a Sunday on the banks of the Amazon River. What's new has no regard (or respect) for natural time, circadian rhythms, geography, or protocol.

Far from overloading her, endless information seems to play on Lisa's vulnerability to want even more information. In his book, *Too Big To Know*, David Weinberger notes,

> "As the amount of information has overloaded the overload, we have not suffered from information anxiety, information tremors, or information butterflies in the stomach. Information overload has become a different sort of problem. It is a cultural condition, maybe experienced individually...it is the fear that we are not getting enough of the information we need."[7]

Lisa is not an Internet addict. She does not neglect her family or her responsibilities by living on the computer but she is painfully aware of what she has to pass up because information is endless. And it causes her some measure of anxiety. But most of all, because time is not expanding at the rate of information, Lisa's informational pursuits squeeze her day. The more time she spends on endless information, the less she has for everything else.

Endless Interruption

For Lisa and her cohorts who live in the Era of Endless, information is abundance. It is like a rich orchard ripe with potential, opportunity, and possibility—POP for short. Search the word "abundance" on Google and over a million hits result in a mere 0.07 seconds. No librarian can compete. But even efficiency can be overwhelming. "We seem to be making the cultural choice...to prefer to start with abundance rather than curation. We include it all."[8]

Another feature of information is that it comes with a sense of urgency, separate and apart from the content of the information itself. Rings, bings, tones and vibrations, screen messages and alerts fight for Lisa's attention announcing the arrival of POP. As a digital native, Lisa prefers to lose some measure of concentration in order to gain POP. POP is hard to resist. It is part of "...an ecology of temptation, teasing us forward."[9] Historically, what leads us into temptation is idleness. "Idle hands are the devil's workshop" we've been told. In the Era of Endless, temptations and distractions come not when we are idle but when we are trying to get things done. A LinkedIn survey of May 2012, polled 6,580 professionals like Lisa and Roger worldwide on how well they follow through on their To-Do lists. 89% of respondents said they could not accomplish all the tasks on their daily To-Do lists largely because of distractions by email, impromptu meetings, or phone calls. In the Era of Endless, distractions have become attractions, interruptions are ubiquitous, and temptations are around us all the time.

Endless Work

Lisa sips another coffee on her drive home. Ah! Coffee. That's what she has forgotten to buy. She grabs the tiny Post-it note pad from the car door pocket, jots down "coffee," and sticks it on the rear view mirror. Very old school.

Now adequately caffeinated, Lisa shifts into high personal productivity. She presses a button on the dashboard that converts her emails into voice. She pulls over (yea), goes on the Internet, and orders coffee paying for it with funds she transfers from her bank account to PayPal. Pleased with maximizing her time and minimizing her effort, Lisa drives on. Bing! A text from Roger, "Got the oil changed?" "Yup" she texts back knowing she should not, but justifying it because she is stopped at a red light, now turned green, which initiated just the slightest honk from the driver behind her.

Lisa is working smarter than ever. She has the Internet in her pocket, no longer gets lost, converts text to voice and voice to text, and can shop whenever she wants. When Lisa was 16, President Richard Nixon predicted a 4-day work week in the "not too distant future." When she graduated college, the retirement age was predicted to be 45 years with a 25 hour work week. But the headline streaming across her iPhone tells another story:

"2012—Americans Working 56 Hours Per Week."[10]

Work Creep

Roger is faring no better investing his productivity gains into leisure. As food and beverage manager for a restaurant chain for the past ten years, he's been overseeing menu planning, food equipment maintenance, ordering produce, meat, and other foods, all while carefully staying on budget. Apps simplify his work by allowing him to be totally mobile. He can order the most seasonally fresh foods from his car, monitor equipment maintenance from home, and move from restaurant to restaurant, without missing a beat. The good side is it gives him the flexibility to spend time with his daughter Emma, squeeze in a quick workout during the day, or meet Lisa for a fast lunch.

On the other hand, he is endlessly accessible to his boss, suppliers, vendors, inspectors, accountants, and the workers he supervises who contact him incessantly. There are conference calls on the weekends and Skype calls at night to other time zones. Roger feels always on, a sense of ceaselessly working in a life without down-time. He is tethered, albeit wirelessly, to screens and machines so that even his most efficient days spill over into the night.

Roger is a victim of work creep. The point of working smarter is to generate a leisure dividend—creating time to stop working and engage in non-work activities. But work efficiencies and personal productivity yield not more leisure, but more work. Every hour of the day seems like fair game. With all the productivity tools he has, why is he not generating a leisure dividend?

Work creep is lengthening Roger's work day. Whatever gains he accrues by maximizing effect and minimizing effort, he loses to work creep. Smartphones, tablets, and other mobile devices bleed his work time into personal time tethering him to his job even during off hours.

Roger's friend Bob commiserates; in fact, Bob is suing the city for overtime. He's a health inspector. The barrage of emails, texts, and calls continue until ten at night, and the expectation is that Bob respond to them within hours. It pulls him away from mowing the lawn, his son's soccer game, and family dinners and he doesn't get paid for this invisible overtime. The city argues that each communication requires less than 15 minutes and they are intermittent, and therefore the time is insignificant. In the Era of Endless, the newest plaintiff is the worker with a wireless device.[11]

The knowledge worker of the Era of Endless is also different from those like Todd, Elly's dad, who worked in an office in the 1970s. Like

Todd, Roger still uses his brain and the computer to organize his work for the most productivity. Like Todd, nobody sets up Roger's day, lays out his tools, or clocks him in. But because Todd was not yet connected to the Internet and accessible 24/7, projects and tasks could be prioritized. Some would remain in the background while others were completed in the foreground. Roger has no such luxury. POP brings a sense of urgency to all tasks and projects that obscures priorities. Everything comes to the foreground at once, putting him always in crisis mode.

During actual crises, such as natural disasters when medical resources are scarce or limited, a form of prioritizing, called triage, is implemented. It is crucial to quickly assess the injured based on who might benefit most from the immediate care that is available, however limited. In the Era of Endless, time is a limited resource. Tasks and To-Dos have to be triaged, and quickly assessed as to which might benefit (get done) in the limited time available. In the Era of Endless, triaging is a new organizing skill.

Home offers some respite from endlessly working. Lisa opens her tablet and shows Roger the latest Facebook family updates and photos. Sitting together on the couch, clicking away at the devices in their laps, is actually kind of nice. They need not talk but they feel close like women in a quilting circle. Emma plays with her dolls. Sometimes digital breaks are the only kind of break Lisa and Roger can manage. Elly and Todd disapprove. Their view of home life is more traditional. The home, they would agree,

> "...has traditionally been a shelter from the crowd, within which human beings experienced life in a different way from how it was experienced on the outside...home has always offered privacy, quiet, and solitude...it also afforded an intimate sort of togetherness that's possible only in shared isolation."[12]

Lisa and Roger, if so inclined, would argue that digital leisure can also reflect togetherness. In the Era of Endless when work is portable and non-stop, people find downtime and breaks wherever and whenever they can. Mixing digital leisure with non-virtual, real-time leisure unmediated by screens is a new organizing skill.

Lack of Closure

Roger experiences a constant, low-level frustration of not ever being able to finish something—anything—start to finish. It doesn't matter how hard he plans his work or works his plan, there is always an interruption knocking his train-of-thought right off the track or a distraction from a task-at-hand. Work has become fragmented, characterized by "...highly interruptible activities loosely hung together unconstrained by time or location."[13] The expectation of interrupttion is built right into the work day practically guaranteeing that projects and tasks remain incomplete. Roger spends his time parrying calls, counter-parrying emails, and thrusting at texts all day long.

Lunge as he might it is an unfair fight. A barrage of distractions, interruptions, and temptations pierce right through Roger's armor of concentration. Each informational missive, hard or soft, demands his time, if only long enough to determine how much more of his time it requires. He would love to begin a task and have the satisfaction of seeing it through, hitting the target with a triumphant touché...take that...finis.

The quest for closure is a human need as old as the checkmark. Finishing things, getting things done from beginning to end, is becoming more elusive. Distractions pull Roger away from a task-at hand. Interruptions disrupt his train-of-thought. The result is what David Allen of *Getting Things Done* fame calls "open loops."

Open loops can undermine quality of life because task incomepletion raises stress. Roger rapidly switches between tasks as many as 36 times an hour, or more than once every two minutes. On his web browser, he keeps three or four tabs open at a time. Studies show that "homo distractus" (people who jump from a task-at-hand to reading emails and back again throughout the day) are in a state of "high alert."

Physically, Roger is pumping cortisol into his system and may be increasing his heart rate. This state of perpetual multitasking might be conditioning Roger to be reactive to just about any stimuli that comes into range. "Multitasking can extend to other stimuli, conditioning the brain to react to immediate opportunities almost as if they are threats, with a squirt of dopamine." Instead of focusing on the task-at-hand, the brain now wants to always switch to the next new thing. It waits in anticipation of POP.[14]

Recovery Time

Closure also eludes Roger because of an organizational issue called "recovery time."[15] Recovery time refers to the time and concentration required to get back to an original task after an interruption. It can take Roger five to twenty minutes to recover, depending on the nature of the interruption and the original task he was attending to. More disconcerting is that there can be two intervening tasks on the path back to the original task. But what Roger finds most interruptive is the change in his physical environment. When he has to open a new window on his computer or go to a website in order to answer somebody's question, that's the Era of Endless analogy to a physical disruption. It's as disruptive as someone tossing tangible documents onto his desk. When his physical environment changes, it's even harder for Roger to reconstruct where he left off.

Endless Connectedness

Another reason Lisa and Roger are long on busy and short on leisure is endless connectedness. At home, Lisa opens up the floodgates of what's new. Facebook brings her photos of smiling family, greetings from friends all over the country, and little grandnieces she has never met dancing in videos. Lisa is very grateful. Without Facebook and social media, she might never enjoy these experiences. In the Era of Endless, being in touch has come to mean never being out of touch.

Along with her everyday non-virtual activities, Lisa has a load of new digital activities. She follows blogs, comments on blogs, joins in LinkedIn group conversations, sets up and reads Google Alerts, and communicates with friends, family and fans. These digital activities sop up whatever non-virtual downtime Lisa has. In a day already short on discretionary time, these virtual activities can displace real-time with family, personal time, or time spent away from a screen or device.

Lisa is becoming a time thief. She finds herself on her iPhone at the park with Emma, stealing time away from the child. "Mommy, watch me." Of course, Lisa does, but her attention is always divided. While celebrating her parent's anniversary last week at a restaurant, she steals time to respond to just one more text. "You can never be too rich or too thin," Gloria Vanderbilt (and other rich, thin women) said. In the Era of Endless you can never be too connected.

Decision-Making

Historically, getting organized has meant being discerning, selective, or particular about our information and our stuff. We used to take the time to make decisions about what we liked and discarded what we did not; we decided what we needed and got rid of what was excess. In the Era of Endless, discernment is practiced far less than in the past.

For instance, Lisa's family and friends send her albums of scores of digital photos. She downloads tantalizing movies and music that she just might enjoy, though she is not yet sure. The process of choosing, of discerning, between the ones she likes and the ones she does not, which to keep and which to delete, is out of reach. It takes three seconds to decide if an image should be kept or deleted. A movie, video, or music takes longer. Multiplied by hundreds of images, beats, and bytes this task suddenly becomes time-consuming.

Lisa has nearly 400 emails she believes she will "go back and process someday." Endless information has found a home in the endless storage capacity of the cloud, truly a marriage made in heaven. That's where Lisa's backlog of emails lives, along with a huge quantity of music, photos, and videos.

"So what?" would be a justified response of a digital native to a digital immigrant. Maybe discernment is irrelevant. "There is so much available storage, we don't have to make decisions anymore," says neuropsychologist David D. Nowell, who specializes in attention issues in Worcester, Massachusetts. "The problem isn't that it slows down your computer—it slows down your brain," he warns.

We don't yet know if failing to make decisions about what is valuable and what is junk, what is important and what is trivial, or what is worthwhile and what is crap has any effect on decision-making in general. We do know that, like off-site self-storage containers, the likelihood of addressing information that is out-of-sight-out-of-mind diminishes. For those who are motivated to be proactive about the disposition of their stored information, strong routines will be required because cues, like maxed out hard-drives, are gone and are not coming back.

Remembering versus Forgetting

Interestingly, social media allows Lisa to share memories in which she did not even participate. Most of the information she depends on does not come from personal observation or direct experiences. In Elly's day, "Mass media fosters the construction of a common shared memory beyond what people have witnessed together…and beyond the narrow confines of geographic proximity."[16]

Elly remembers, as do most people her age, precisely where she was during the Kennedy assassination and the moon landing. Today, the Internet affords the same kind of shared memory. Lisa remembers 9/11 and the horrendous school shooting in Newtown, Connecticut. She does not remember all the events of the year or the decade or even of the past several days, and that's the way it should be.

Forgetting is the default, remembering the exception. By saving most of her emails Lisa is exemplifying an Era of Endless practice. Remembering is the default and forgetting is the exception.[17] Of course, she is not actually remembering the content of each email, but in failing to delete them, she is choosing not to forget them, not to let them decline into irrelevancy and go the way of most past information.

In the popular TV show of the 1960s called *Mission Impossible* the secret agents would receive their mission by listening to a cassette tape, a high-tech device of the day. To keep the mission a secret from counter-spies and bad guys, the tape concluded with the words, "This tape will self-destruct in ten seconds," whereupon the tape would ignite and burn inside the cassette player rendering it useless.

Viktor Mayer-Schonberger, the author of *Delete*, predicts that future devices will permit the creator of information to automatically program the destruction of information.[18] Lisa has no such self-destruct mechanism. Getting organized in the Era of Endless may well require a step-up in the skills of "forgetting" to include deleting, archiving, and shredding.

Pull-Back

Maybe the last straw was the relentless parade of TV, Internet, and radio ads announcing that Walmart will open at 8 PM on Thanksgiving night. Maybe it was cumulative. Whatever it was, Lisa turned to Roger and said with total conviction, "We have got to get away." Away, she declared, from the screens and machines and the interruptions and the distractions. He immediately knew she was right. They had reached the point where:

> "In barely one generation we've moved from exulting in the time-saving devices that have so expanded our lives to trying to get away from them—often in order to make more time. The more ways we have to connect, the more many of us seem desperate to unplug. Like teenagers, we appear to have gone from knowing nothing about the world to knowing too much all but overnight."[19]

Roger and Lisa agree to take a short vacation, nothing too complicated, just a place with lots of sunshine, lots of outdoor activities, and a chance to be away from the screens and machines. It's March. They shoot for a May vacation, giving them plenty of time to plan.

At work, Roger is a planner. His job as a food and beverage manager requires him to plan ahead. He has to figure out restaurant menus months in advance with consideration for local, seasonal farm foods. He plans just-in-time delivery of produce for freshness. He projects costs and cash flow. But when it comes to his personal life, instant gratification has ruled the day: jumping on a Groupon offer for a next-day discounted golf game, knocking off a quick game of Angry Birds, or having a spontaneous drink with his buddy Bob. Roger finds thinking ahead to leisure time something that takes a bit getting used to. He and Lisa lie in bed and practice imagining the beach and the warmth of the sun. They rarely spend time using their imagination and it is rusty. And actually being on vacation? Roger and Lisa's daily life proves they can do three things at once but can they do just one? Can they just relax?

They set about planning their vacation and run headlong into an Era of Endless hazard. Endless information can being bring decision-making to its knees. Lisa sets up a dozen Google Alerts for vacation spots from Florida to California, and is inundated with information. Roger jumps into travel site chats and LinkedIn conversations; it's all helpful but a lot to absorb. Lisa talks to her online friends, fans, and family about vacation spots. The more information she gathers, the more confused she gets. Roger subscribes to several online newsletters and blogs and prints out tons of information. Then there are the State Department travel advisories to check, the barrage of travel bargains and offers to review, and live travel agents to speak with. It's now April and they have not decided where to go. Lisa and Roger can't see the proverbial forest through the trees.

With all the information they have amassed, something is missing. Pull back. In the Era of Endless when information is endless and choices are unlimited, pull back is the new organizing skill. Pull back is stepping away from information so that judgment can be applied. Although there are many choices, there can only be one decision.

Information Afterlife

The deed is done. Roger and Lisa buy tickets for Phoenix, Arizona. Elly and Todd will take care of granddaughter Emma at Lisa's house because it is Emma's first time away from her parents; it will be easier if she is in her own home and sleeps in her own bed. To stay connected to Emma, Lisa insists Elly learn FaceTime, a web-based program that connects people computer-to-computer with video and audio. Emma will be able to see and talk to her parents while they are away.

"Can't she just talk to you on the phone?" Elly complains. "It's good for Emma to learn to be away from her parents, otherwise she'll have separation anxiety all her life," Elly protests in her best counseling voice. Elly has deliberately avoided learning to use Twitter, she very occasionally updates her Facebook page, and she texts only when it's faster than a call, but she has been reluctant to fully engage every new Internet innovation. She loses the fight, learns FaceTime, and thankfully, finds it easy to use.

As the time for the vacation approaches Lisa begins to worry what would happen if the plane went down. Emma will lose both parents. The odds are small, so Roger and Lisa decide not to change their tickets and travel separately, but they do meet with an attorney, and draw up a Will and other end-of-life documents. In Elly's day, a safe deposit box and an executor pretty much assured that when someone died or was incapacitated valuables could be accessed and assets distributed.

What is unique to the Era of Endless is that information has an afterlife. Roger and Lisa have passwords and user codes for automated deposits, withdrawals, and payments. They have passwords for websites, accounts, and the files on their computer. Nobody else knows the passwords. They are not recorded anywhere. Their Facebook pages will live long after they are gone unless they do something to stop it. In the Era of Endless, contending with the afterlife of information is a new organizing skill.

"Your Dad and I have a Will," Elly informs them. "We leave all our worldly goods to you and Roger." Holy crap, Lisa thinks to herself as she and Roger get in the cab to go to the airport. All their worldly goods? Elly and Todd have downsized but they still have a lot of stuff. Anyway, it's not something Lisa can think about now.

Endless Stuff

Emma cries when the cab leaves and her grandparents distract her with toys. Emma has a lot of toys. According to a recent ethno-archeological study undertaken by UCLA's Center on Everyday Lives of Families, Emma is typical. "Each new child in a household leads to a 30 percent increase in a family's inventory of possessions during the preschool years alone."[20] Clothes, toys, dolls, trophies, crafts, games, books and electronics proliferate. The study concludes that busy parents trade in time with the kids for time the kids can spend with their toys. And like the Boomers that preceded them, Lisa's generation works hard. Materially providing for the children (and themselves) is a reward for never-ending work.

While Emma plays, Elly wanders around Lisa's house noticing the technology gizmos and gadgets scattered about. Instead of fruit in the fruit bowl on the dining room table there is a buffet of cell phones, remote controls, ear buds, and various cables. In the bedroom are Frankenstein boxes of older electronics: cameras, radios, headphones, walkmans, telephones, adapters, and cords with plugs. Though none are older than ten years they're already considered relics. Elly wonders why Lisa doesn't recycle them. Surely she's set a good example for her. She has many fond memories schlepping plastic bottles, aluminum cans, newspapers, and other disposables to the recycling center. As a child, Lisa would carefully sort clear plastic soda bottles from green ones and put them into the huge recycling bins that dwarfed her, making her seem even smaller than she was.

Elly is unaware that Lisa is trying to be responsible about the end-less quantities of electronics, each with eternal components that never decompose. They're perpetually being replaced with later models and versions. At a recent Earth Day event, Lisa read literature explaining that charities like Goodwill Industries receive millions of pounds of electronics a year. Most of them are unusable. The charities are stuck with them and their solution is to often export the electronics to China, India, and Africa. Little children with hammers smash the mother-boards to smithereens and in the process are directly exposed to toxins from the electronics that damage their liver and brain.[21] The toxins in electronics can leach into the groundwater of landfills and cause health problems.

Rather than participate in this tragedy, Lisa keeps the electronics out of the landfill, out of the recycling stream, and inside her home, knowing full well this is not the best solution for herself, her home, or the planet. In the Era of Endless, taking responsibility for electronics through their entire lifecycle, is a new skill for coping with the rapid obsolescence of toxic devices that cannot be returned to the earth.

CONCLUSION

The Era of Endless is remarkable. Information, free and abundant, is accessible without regard to age, education, station in life, or the logistics of geography or time zone. It is a gift like the oceans and the sky. Earning a living or working hard at anything—a hobby, a project or a pastime—is nearly boundless because it is facilitated by easy communication and collaboration, can be conducted anywhere and at any time, and is unrestrained by buildings and bosses. Potential opportunities and possibilities abound and there has never been more ways to learn of their existence, take advantage of their benefits, and prosper. When we want stuff, we are undeterred by banks, store hours, or our wallet. And there are plenty of off-site storage units for everyone!

Getting organized in the Era of Endless will allow us to take advantage of its remarkable gifts by coping with its excesses, managing the side effects, and mitigating the downside of endless information, stuff, interruption, and work.

New organizing skills, and new spins on traditional skills appropriate to the Era of Endless, are explained in Parts Three through Six. It will be a challenge. But as we have seen in prior eras, getting organized can lead to a more fully realized life, a life where the distance between the goals of who we are, what we want, and where we are going is moved ever and ever closer.

---

[1] *Too Big To Know,* pg. 5.
[2] Caterina Fake, *Fear of Missing Out and Social Media,* blog post, March 15, 2011
[3] Gary Small, Director of UCLA's Memory & Aging Research Center, Internet interview 2011.
[4] Princeton and Stanford University, *The Pursuit of Useless Information,* 2011
[5] *Too Big to Know,* pg 38
[6] FileHeads Professional Organizer, *A Survey of Information Artifacts,* 2011
[7] *Too Big to Know,* pg. 9
[8] *Too Big to Know,* pg. 176

⁹ *Too Big to Know*, pg. 117

¹⁰ Bureau of Labor Statistics, *American Time Use Study,* 2011

¹¹ Paul Davidson, "More American Workers Sue Employers Over Overtime Pay," *USA Today,* April, 2012

¹² *Hamlet's Blackberry,* pg. 178

¹³ KPMG study, "Work Fragmentation: How Much Is Too Much," 2010

¹⁴ Mozilla Firefox Web Browser Report, 2012

¹⁵ Dr. Gloria Mark, *The Cost of Interrupted Work: More Speed and Stress,* University of California, Irvine, 2010

¹⁶ *Hamlet's Blackberry,* pg. 153

¹⁷ Viktor Mayer-Schonberger, *Delete: The Virtue of Forgetting in the Digital Age*

¹⁸ *Delete,* pg. 171

¹⁹ Pico Iyer, "The Joy of Quiet," *New York Times,* December, 2011

²⁰ UCLA, Center on Everyday Lives of Families (CELP) "Life at Home in the 21st Century," 2012

²¹ "The Basel Ban: A Triumph for Global Environmental Justice," Briefing Paper, October, 2011

ERA OF ENDLESS
PART
THREE

WHAT TO DO WHEN INFORMATION IS ENDLESS AND TIME IS NOT

THE OLD DONE

There's no escaping the fact that information is endless and time is not. You need a new way to satisfy your informational needs while embracing two realities:

- there will always be more information to pursue, and
- there will never be enough time to pursue it

In prior eras, there was no actual doctrine called The Old Done, but if there were it would be characterized by facts that finalized your queries, comprehensiveness that exhausted your curiosity, and information that stayed up-to-date longer than the time it took to find it. In the Era of Endless information, comprehensiveness broadens and deepens every day making the quest for it Quixote-like. Facts still exist but there are countless counterfacts to consider. And information obsolescence is faster than ever. You need a New Done because the Old Done doesn't fit in the Era of Endless.

THE NEW DONE

The New Done doesn't mean the information you seek, save, or use should be superficial or out-of-date. It does mean that you honor your informational commitments to yourself and others without endless information robbing you of the time you need for living a life of quality.

The New Done has three major parts.

1. Dealing with information turn-on
2. Identifying and yielding to stopping points
3. Setting "done" ahead of time

1. Does Information Turn You On?

We know that endlessly abundant and free information can be a real turn-on. And that's not a bad thing. There are many positive qualities: the thrill of the hunt for information is exciting, searching on the Internet is fun, finding what you're looking for is satisfying, and getting into a focused flow is productive.

But being over-stimulated by endlessly abundant information has a dark side, too. If you're really hooked on information, it can undermine your quality of life by stealing time from your family and other critical non-screen-oriented activities. The *process* of searching for, finding, and amassing information leaves little time for the *purpose* of the information whether it is to draw a conclusion, complete a report, inform a decision, or answer a question. This can lead to missed deadlines, delayed deliverables, and useless information because it comes too late.

How Much Are You Turned On By Information?

Answer Yes or No to the following to see the extent that information turns you on:

1.	I tend to jump from website to website.	Yes	No
2.	I sometimes have as many as five website/tabs open at a time.	Yes	No
3.	I click on a link, then another, and another. Five is not uncommon.	Yes	No
4.	I lose track of time.	Yes	No
5.	I go on tangents to off-topic but interesting information.	Yes	No
6.	I don't know when I am done or finished.	Yes	No

If you answered Yes to Questions 1, 2, and 3, you definitely are turned on by information. Endless information is tough for you to control. The best strategy for you is to *increase* information pushed to you and *decrease* information you pull. Two ways to push information to you are Real Simple Syndication (RSS) and Google Alerts.

- Go to the websites you find most useful and click on the RSS feed button. Thereafter, whenever that website updates content the information will come to you rather than you going out and getting it.
- Go to Google Alerts and type in keywords that interest you. Updates on those topics will be sent to your inbox.

When information is pushed to you, you can cut back on surfing the Internet so much.

If you answered Yes to Question 4, you may lose track of time because information is so captivating and so interesting that you leave the temporal world. The best way to come back is to set an alarm. Alarms are everywhere: in your computer, on your iPad and smartphone, on your clocks, and your oven, maybe even on your wristwatch. Set an alarm for one hour. When it rings, check to be sure your search is on course and you haven't become tangled in the web and forgotten to pick your children up from school.

If you answered Yes to Question 5, you're likely a sucker for serendipitous information. You bump into serendipitous information along the way; although it is interesting, it is tangential to your major focus. My client, Rhonda, is susceptible to tangents and serendipitous information. In the process of researching ultra-light laptops versus the iPad for traveling, she bumped into information about ergonomics, the resale value of iPads, and how to take her computer through airport security—all cool stuff but it gobbled up her time.

Figure out where to offload serendipitous and tangential information. Rhonda tags it and dumps it into Evernote so she can access it later if she needs it. Another option is to properly title the information and save it to your hard drive or a flash drive. The idea is to get it out of your way so you can refocus.

If you answered Yes to Question 6, the solution is to pull-back periodically. My client Frank needed to buy a new car. While researching, he amassed huge amounts of information including downloaded documents, hardcopy brochures from dealerships, and online classified ads. He spoke with friends, family and fans, used social media, and chatted with owners of the same make of vehicles he was considering. But the more information he amassed the more confused he became. I encouraged him to take two hours to pull-back, step away from all the information, and review it from the vantage point of his ten must-have car features. Pull-back gave him the chance to eliminate information and, more importantly, to impose his judgment on his information. Information can provide you with choices, but it's your own judgment and preferences that will result in a decision.

2. Stopping Points

The second part to The New Done is stopping points. Even if information is not a turn-on for you, it's still challenging to know when to stop informational pursuits. In the past, stopping was governed by library hours, availability of relevant information, intractable facts, and the voices of experts. Because information now is never-ending, there is a new set of stopping points.

Stop when your information is well-rounded. A search is functionally well-rounded when quality information from a variety of sources is combined. Of course, this varies with your topic, but once information is well-rounded you can stop. That might mean including information from people who have something in common with you *and* those who are very different from you. It could include information from a wide range of sources like chats, websites, blogs, podcasts, articles, and live experts. Well-rounded might mean using information that is real-time and some that is historical. Instead of thinking of information only in terms of the depth or breadth, think of it as an orb. When your orb of information is well-rounded, then you can stop.

Stop when you have formed your own opinion, conclusion, or decision. There is no end to the amount of information you can gather from others. Points of views, perspectives, arguments, counter-arguments, facts, claims, and prior research may all be relevant and worth considering in your search or research. At some point, however, you may need to draw your own conclusion, formulate an opinion, or make a decision. These are great stopping points.

Stop and point. Another way to stop is to become a great pointer. No informational pursuit will ever be complete, but when you've done your best, point readers to great sources of additional information. Depending on the specifics of your topic, that could be bibliographies, websites, links, books, live experts, blogs, footnotes, source material, or any number of other sources.

Stop when the amount of information is in proportion to its importance or consequence. Scale the amount of information you gather in proportion to the importance or the consequence of its purpose. You might dedicate more time researching holistic cures for reflux disorder than where to take your out-of-town visitors to dinner. Choosing a summer camp for your kids deserves more informational time than looking up how to get grass stains out of jeans.

3. Set Done Ahead Of Time

The third part of the New Done is a little counter-intuitive. It calls for setting *done* ahead of time. It's easy to go on and on informationally-speaking, not only because information is stimulating, but also because there's so much of it. It seems that there is always just a little more useful or interesting information. And there is! There's no end to it. So determining when you're done is not always clear.

I work with my clients to set *done* ahead of time. In other words, I encourage them to find the qualitatively best information in a quanti-tative set of parameters. Let me give you an example: My client, Veronica, is a blogger for one of the largest apartment management companies in America. She blogs about the apartment lifestyle on subjects like how to buy renter's insurance, understanding pet clauses in leasing agreements, pool courtesy, and other topics of interest to apartment dwellers. "I'm a good writer, but I'm an information hound," Veronica tells me. "I could lose my job if I don't become more productive. I never know when I'm done." I discovered Veronica spends as much as six hours researching for a 500 word blog. Veronica and I found an app that sets an alarm to go off at a certain word count, in this case 400. When the alarm goes off, Veronica is aware she has just 100 more words she can write.

I put her on a website diet of up to three highly authoritative websites. To round out her research, she uses LinkedIn Groups to gather information. Veronica can now do two blogs in the time it used to take to do one, and she never misses a deadline.

Information overkill confronts Veronica at home, too. "I'm looking into summer camps for my kids. It's taking hours and hours and the application deadline is coming up," she tells me. We set *done* this way: look only at camps in her budget range, limit the choices to five, put them out to social networking for feedback for one week, and then make a choice.

Setting *done* ahead of time is a tactic that starts by asking the questions that help design quantitative parameters to your qualitative search or research.

Questions to Set Done Ahead Of Time

- Is someone waiting for this information? When exactly do they need it?
- Does the information need to be introductory or in-depth?
- Is there a specific word count, page count, or other parameter?
- Can I point to additional resources if I run out of time?
- Do I need to move things around in my schedule to accommodate this informational project?
- Is the deadline or due date negotiable?

Getting Organized in the Era of Endless

Don't hesitate to make up your own parameters if you have none to work with. If you are gathering information for someone else and there is no clear deadline, ask for a time limit. Give some thought to the depth or scope of the information required before you head out onto the Internet. Maybe you need to go long instead of deep or deep instead of long. If you have a lot going on and you have to take on an informational project, look at your schedule and plot out dedicated times for working on the project so other obligations aren't neglected.

Implementing The New Done by assessing how much information turns you on, identifying and yielding to stopping points, and setting *done* ahead of time will serve you well when information is endless and time is not.

COPING WITH KEEPING UP

Keeping up (also called FOMO, Fear of Missing Out) is not new. It's been a classic rationalization for the drive to find and save information in all eras. But now that information is endless and relentless, keeping up can be psychologically burdensome. The Harvard Education blog in 2010 noted "...the feeling of overload comes not just from the time-suck of information exploration but from the sense of obligation that accompanies it...it is all too common to feel constantly behind: constantly in need of keeping up."

Although keeping up is not new, the stressful sense of obligation and an anxious feeling of constantly being behind are new. Keeping-up anxiety is most evident with emails and social media. The evidence is overwhelming, especially among digital natives, people born in the 1980s and 1990s.

- A Pew Internet Report published in 2012 reports that 44% of cell owners have slept with their phone next to their bed because they did not want to miss calls, texts, or other updates during the night.
- According to a University of Chicago study released in 2012, tweeting or checking email may be harder to resist than cigarettes and alcohol.

- Larry Rosen, the author of *iDisorder*, studied the iGeneration (born in the 1990s) and the Net Generation (born in the 1980s). His study reports that both groups become anxious if unable to check text messages several times daily.

Keeping up applies not only to current events and news, but also to keeping up with each other—our families, and friends. Email and social media (and to an increasing extent, Twitter) are the most popular ways to keep up in the Era of Endless, totally outrunning older forms of keeping up like phone calls, newspapers, radio, and TV. The four reasons my clients endlessly check and accumulate email are:

- concern that it may be urgent
- the use of email as a To-Do list
- the use of email as a filing cabinet, and
- checking email frequently has simply become a habit.

If you can relate, here is what to do to exert a bit of mindful discipline on email.

I Need to Keep Up With Email Because it May Be Urgent. Raise your standard for what is considered urgent. Words that describe "urgent" include "crucial," "imperative," "pressing," and "requiring immediate attention." Does your notion of urgency rise to these descriptions? The current expectation for a response to email averages 48 hours. If you change your standard of urgent, you will change other people's expectations as well. If someone wants your attention quickly, they'll likely call or text. Practice checking and responding to email five times a day or less. An added bonus for checking emails less frequently is that processing emails in batches is more efficient than bouncing around from computer work to emails to errands to emails to reading to emails and so forth.

I Need to Keep Up With Email Because Email is My To-Do list. If it is your practice to keep emails in your inbox as your To-Do list, be wary. Not only is it easy to overlook a message, you may also feel so overwhelmed that taking action is difficult. Instead, learn to turn an action-oriented email into a task. Visit the Practical Hacks website to learn how to do that in Outlook: www.tinyurl.com/7kf252f

Another tip is to turn the subject line of the message into a verb and re-save it. For instance, the subject line "Robin's Wedding" can be changed to "RSVP to Robin's Wedding." Now you know what you must **do** with the email, not just what it is about. You can also save it to a folder called "Take Action." If you don't think you'll check your folders regularly, stick with using a subject line verb instead of a noun.

I Need to Keep Up With Email Because Email is My Filing Cabinet. Fine. But do you just dump documents in your filing cabinet? No. You put your documents into file folders. Do that with your email too. Basic folders like "Committee Minutes," "Very Important," "Archive" or "Take Action" can be extremely helpful to cull an overflowing inbox. Filing emails by sender is the strongest determinant of an email's importance so if you want to be sure an email from your boss doesn't get mixed in with an email from your sister, file it by sender.

I Need to Keep Up With Email Because It's a Habit. Habits are good things; They economize time by allowing us to repeat actions or behaviors in the same circumstances to get the same result or outcome. Opening email the very first thing in the morning is a habit best reserved for people who can quickly scan their email and determine what needs immediate attention. If that is not you, here is a better habit to form. Before you look at your emails in the morning, close something first. Finish something from the day before. Then open your email. Once you open your email inbox all kinds of new work begs for your attention and you never get to finish something you already started.

SOCIAL MEDIA RULES OF ENGAGEMENT

Social media is a broadcast media, a way to connect, a platform for interaction, a tool for community-building, a marketing vehicle, a means of communication, and a disseminator of information. It's a big player in the world of endless information and can be a huge time-suck, so it's worthy of your intentional effort to rein it in to support your purposes rather than deplete your time.

Keeping up, being in the know, and staying on top of what's new has a price. The continuous partial attention that social media can produce "...creates an always on, anywhere, anytime, anyplace behavior that creates an artificial sense of crisis. We are always on high alert. We reach to keep a top priority in focus, while, at the same time, scanning the periphery to see if we are missing other opportunities."[1]

Rules of Engagement

- Develop a routine for your participation. A fixed day of the week and regular time of the day will make you less reactive to the beck and call of social media. Do more if it's satisfying, enjoyable, and suits your purpose.

- Avoid jumping on every social media bandwagon. With the proliferation of platforms (Instagram, Google+, and Pinterest were born just yesterday in Internet-life terms and more arise everyday), shed a platform.

- Be helpful and bring value when you use social media. Provide insight and direction without rambling, being ridiculously self-serving, or salesy.

- Be concise.

- Be consistent with messaging—consistency counts more than frequency. If people follow you, don't let them down.

- Use TweetDeck, HootSuite, or Buffer to schedule posts, tweets, and status updates across several platforms at once; but there's no need to post every hour.

- Dedicate regular time for responding to deserving replies and comments. It's the social part of social media. However, you cannot—and should not—respond to all replies and comments.

- Be choosy about the groups you join. LinkedIn and other social media channels have redundant groups. There's no need to join all of them.

- Have real-time, live friends, fans, and followers, too.

- Remember, missing out and choosing to not keep up can also bring joy.

Special Twitter Tips

- Be selective about who you follow and be willing to unfollow your mentor/hero/guru/teacher/favorite celebrity. Your favorite today will replaced by somebody new tomorrow. Don't just keep piling on. Add one : Drop one is a good ratio.
- If you haven't replied to a tweet within 12 hours, then don't.
- Add to the conversation to further it along. If you have nothing to add, there's no need to tweet.
- Don't thank those who sign up to follow you unless you have something specific to say to them.

No measure of advice or number of tips can substitute for being true to your purpose. If your purpose for engaging in social media is no-holds-barred-my-time-is-your-time, more power to you. If your purpose is more focused, such as regular contact with family and friends, increasing your visibility, positioning yourself as an expert, or deliberately going after customers, contacts, or clients, there's much you can do to bring down the high alert and *always on* nature of social media.

FILTERING AND PURGING— A NEW ORGANIZING SKILL

When information is endless and time is not, filtering and purging (F&P) is crucial to maximize effect and minimize effort; in fact, F&P together have become a new, crucial organizing skill. Though information follows no typical life-cycle in general, it usually has a point of creation, undergoes usage, and from there it can be shared, saved, or any of a number of options.

In the Era of Endless, filtering reduces excess information at the front end while purging completes the cycle at the back end. Purging moves the clutter, the unwanted, and the unneeded information out of your way. You'll know what you have, will be able to find what you need, and spend less time searching and retrieving.

Philosophically, F&P can be understood as a healthy way of forgetting in a society that enables us to remember (save) information forever.

Winning the battle against endless information can be accomplished by using several purging techniques: deleting, shredding, scanning, archiving, and purging-by-output. Few of us use more than one or two of these methods, but the complete arsenal of purging techniques will prevent endless, excess, and unneeded information from sopping up your precious time.

Deleting

Scientists predict that in the future, many kinds of information will have an embedded expiration date with the capacity to self-delete.

> "One possible way we can mimic human forgetting in the digital realm is by associating information we store in digital memory with expiration dates that users set. Our digital storage devices would be made to automatically delete information that has reached or exceeded its expiry date...it will likely have a manual override to extend it."[2]

Well, totally automatic self-delete is not quite here but you can take advantage of some semi-automatic weapons. Karen Simon, a professsional organizer with extensive technology expertise, advises that you can set up:

- email programs to archive or expire messages at a future date. When a message ages to that date, it is moved out of your inbox or deleted altogether.
- rules to delete messages from specific people or with certain words in the subject line. Search "auto delete old files" in your browser for more information.
- regular calendar reminders to alert you to manually delete files.

"Setting up files to automatically delete can be tricky," Simon warns. "Without clear file naming conventions and labels, you could delete a message by accident or remove a file somebody else needs."

Deleting is certainly nothing new, but in the Era of Endless it pays to delete more often than in the past because of rapid information obsolescence. Information on investing, for instance, can be obsolete eight minutes after it comes off the press—or is posted on the Internet. Health information is available to average consumers rather than just to experts and practitioners, but that means it is up to consumers to monitor that they are using the most current health information.

Just-In-Time Information

In addition to frequent deletions, practice "just-in-time" information. This is a term borrowed from the inventory of agricultural goods. Distributors stock limited supplies of highly perishable agricultural goods to avoid spoilage before being shipped. In the same way, financial, health, and mental health information is best accessed just-in-time so it is fresh when you need to have it, know it, or use it. Keep it handy for ready use, but delete it after the explicit need for the information has passed.

Does The Cloud Make Deleting Irrelevant?

William Powers observes in *Hamlet's Blackberry* that though we are "...physical creatures who perceive and know the world through our bodies...digital information that weighs on us today exists in a *non-physical* medium." We are rapidly getting used to a body of knowledge with no body. With low-cost unlimited storage, and simple retrieval, documents are being saved to the cloud at unprecedented rates. Some people see it as a heavenly solution to deleting. Does the cloud making deleting digital information irrelevant? I put the question to my colleagues who are professional organizers and information technology specialists. They support the continuation of good purging habits, even with the cloud.

Decision-Making Mega-Skill

Why is deleting important even though we have infinite storage in the cloud? Because deleting is an exercise in decision-making. It isn't about how easy or cheap it is to stow in the cloud, it's about using our decision-making muscle. In the Era of Endless as in all eras before, decision-making is a still a mega skill. Deciding what you value and what you don't, whether to keep something or not, what's important and what isn't is an ongoing process that is healthy for every aspect of getting organized—and for life in general.

Good decision-making affects not only your information, but also how you decide to spend your time, which interruptions you choose to deal with and those you decide to ignore, and the disposition of all your possessions and stuff. Decision-making keeps you on top of organizing. And it's ongoing. Your needs will change. Your preferences will change. Your life chapters will change. Decision-making, including deleting, is the little engine that could keep you from getting overwhelmed in the Era of Endless.

"I believe younger kids are not learning these skills because they don't have to and nobody is teaching them," notes Simon. Could lax informational decision-making undermine decision-making in other domains of life? Alix Longfellow, a professional organizer who trains people to use technology to get organized, puts it this way, "The act of being critical with the data coming into our lives, whether it is an email, document, or resource, that process of evaluating data helps develop problem-solving skills. So it's not always just about filing or eliminating clutter. It's about developing analytical skills."

Research on the connection between making organizing decisions and decision-making in general does not exist, but IT-trained professional organizers see a trend. They report that clients who fail to delete documents tend to allow their inboxes to overflow, closets to clutter up, garages to go to the dogs, and offices to become overwhelmed with clutter. There might be a trend in education, too. "My students struggle with deciding what information to include and what to leave out of their essays. They find a ton of information on the Internet and load it into their essays but they seem to have great difficulty pruning the irrelevant information," a client who is a junior high school English teacher told me. It will be years before researchers can tell us if our decision-making muscle is becoming lax.

But just because the cloud is convenient, that's no reason *not* to use it. As a matter of fact, I find that some of my digital immigrant clients can be a bit intimidated by the cloud. Rather than overuse it, they tend to underuse it. The reason is that they conflate "control" with "security." It's a bit like fear of flying. Everybody knows that the drive to the airport is far more dangerous than the flight. But because you have lost control of the plane to the pilot, you think you are in more danger than you actually are.

Cloud computing companies are the pilots of today. Every day, all day, their job is to protect your data. They train, secure, maintain, check and train, secure, maintain and check all over again. You're not in control like you would be if your information were on your own computer or server, but in many ways your information is more secure in the hands of professionals than with amateur pilots like yourself. Yes, things can go wrong and you need to take adequate back-up steps. But don't pass up the benefits of the cloud by mistaking control for security.

Home and Personal Retention Schedule

Businesses are not the only enterprises that need retention and destruction schedules. In the Era of Endless, households and individuals require them, too. Much of your personal information doesn't have industry or governmental standards for how long to keep it and when to get rid of it.

Everybody's home and personal papers differ, but not as widely as you might think. Report cards, school records, vaccinations, genealogy, travel documents, family information, and all kinds of information in your personal filing system comes without clear expiration, retention, or destruction guidelines. It's up to you to create a simple home and personal retention schedule.

Professional organizers excel at setting up home and personal filing systems and the retention and destruction schedules that go with them. Find one at www.napo.net. I like the guidelines laid out at Just Organize Your Stuff (www.tinyurl.com/6658wlo). Find other guidelines for personal documentation at www.irs.gov and www.usa.gov.

Go Forward Not Backwards

In the Era of Endless, sometimes there is an inclination to keep stuff in an effort to track or re-create the situation that generated it. For instance, many of my clients keep every merchandise, grocery, and clothing receipt. Their intent is to re-create their expenditures, track them to find out how much they are spending, match them against their statements, or build a budget so they can be better consumers and money managers. When information is endless and time is not, there never seems to be a right time—or enough time—to do this laudable exercise. So the receipts stack up. Reconciling bank statements, reviewing investments, figuring out preventive car maintenance, and other backtracking is nearly impossible in the Era of Endless. It's hard enough to go forward, let alone backwards!

There are better ways than manually tracking, back-tracking, and re-creating. After all, this is the Era of Endless information, with endless apps, software, and web services to simplify your information challenges. Most of these technologies are free, easy to use, and simple to learn. But first you have to identify what you need. That's easy. Take a look around. Are you saving receipts? Got a big box called "Health expenses"? Stacks of ATM receipts? A large wad of bank or investment statements? Holding on to a year's worth of tax stuff? Figure out which information you want to track, monitor, backtrack, and digitize and there's an app for you. Go to the free website, www.Mint.com to track what you spend with your debit and credit cards. It categorizes, helps you build a budget, and plots your expenditures.

Where To Get Help To Track Information

- Turn to somebody you know who tracks information well
- Reach out to a CPA or financial planner
- Call in a professional organizer for advice
- Hire a college kid to scan your hardcopy stuff into digital information
- Check out www.virtualassistants.com
- Find an instruction video on YouTube
- Go the App Store

Shredding

Shredding has an old school feel to it. You take real paper and put it into a real machine with real mechanical parts that really render the information on that paper unreadable. Old school reasons to shred apply to the Era of Endless too, so in that respect not much has changed.

- You like your privacy and want it protected. Putting your papers in recycling bins make it accessible for anybody to see. It's nobody's business what's on your documents.
- Space in your drawers and files and folders is freed up.
- Shredded papers make great gerbil cage liners

What *is* new in the Era of Endless are shredders with the power to easily shred CDs and DVDs as well as paper. Modern paper shredders crosscut so documents can't easily be reassembled, protecting sensitive information from identity thieves. Commercial-grade shredders can eat your hard drive; and it's a good thing because the Era of Endless is marked by identity theft. Identity theft cost households $13.3 billion in 2010 in direct financial losses, according to the Justice Department.

Relevant documents to shred are those with social security and account numbers. The truth is you can't prevent others from getting your name, address, or phone number. The good news is that your name, address, and phone number are not adequate for stealing your identity. Bank, credit card, insurance, and investment account numbers, as well as your social security number, are required. The hottest information for identity thieves is your medical information so they can apply for medical insurance, and tax records to misappropriate your refund, so be sure to give those a good grind in the shredder.

Here's the thing about shredding. It's unlikely you will do it. It's boring and time-consuming, a deadly combination. But because it's important, *somebody* has to do it. Mobile shredding trucks will come to your home office or off-site office depending on the size of your load. They'll destroy it right before your eyes. You can also take shredding to most Office Depot stores and maybe even watch it being shred. Employees may not get to it immediately and it might take quite a while to shred. But there are secure bins where your documents live until the shredding is accomplished.

A small scale shredder that feeds only five pages at time might do the job for you, but once you have a backlog it is harder and harder for you to find the time. Consider using an out-of-work teenager or an intern to do the job. Just be certain they are mindful of shredding hazards, like long hair, shirt cuffs, jewelry, and fingers!

Scanning Documents

Scanning also makes paper go away, but with some added organizational benefits. Like shredding, scanning can be labor intensive but once accomplished it really economizes time. Scanners can extract key information and organize it into a database. For instance, receipts can be searched by amount, vendor, or date; documents by title, author, or keywords. Data that is digitized can also be exported into programs like Excel or QuickBooks or attached to an email.

Most personal printers have a scanning option. Read the manual to find out how your scanner operates.

Technology Filters

Filtering information from your information stream at its source is powerful. In the Era of Endless it's necessary to put as much technology between you and information inundation as possible. Personalized searches based on Facebook data, Amazon's and Google's complex algorithms, and news aggregators like Digg all help filter information selectively. Even Twitter is a kind of filter that enables you to follow people who follow what you are interested in. Real simple syndication (RSS) is a filter for sifting through websites based on your informational preferences. Crowdsourcing using Delicious and Stumble Upon leverages the wisdom of crowds of people with similar interests to filter information for you. Filtering out what you don't need from what you do need is a skill of incredible importance in the Era of Endless.

> "In a digital world, the race goes not to the person with the most information, but the person with the best combination of low-volume and high-relevancy information. The person with the least inputs necessary to maximize output."[3]

Life Chapter Filters

Life chapters are like chapters in a book. Though a story line and characters move from chapter to chapter, a chapter closes and a new one begins. Things move along. Filtering life chapters is a great non-technological way to purge information.

As a professional organizer, I notice that I am often hired to help someone get organized when they are at a juncture in life. When there are changes, one life chapter closes and a new life chapter begins. At the first organizing session, I always ask, "Why are you getting organized **now?** What is changing or transitioning?" Maybe it is a second marriage and they need to meld households. Or it's a job loss and they're setting up a home business to generate income. Perhaps they're retired and need to clear things out to make way for new interests. Could be they're facing a health issue and want stuff to be easier to manage. You can ask these questions of yourself.

Life chapters present great opportunities to filter. You can filter your time commitments, files, and stuff into your new life chapters. This means discarding old chapter information, files and stuff, and organizing those in support of your new chapter. You can even shed old chapter time commitments.

My client Carol is a good example. "I left my teaching job and started a new job as a receptionist in a fitness center. I downloaded important files to a flash drive and gave it to my replacement. I tossed out documents in my desk, being careful to shred the sensitive ones. I cleared my calendar for job training and orientation. I took myself off email distribution lists pertaining to the old job. I cleared out my files and recycled the contents of seventeen 3-ring binders, then I donated the binders to a local school. I made a shadow box of my Teacher of the Year certificate, a few choice photographs and a poem from my students. It hangs in my living room as a loving reminder of my teaching career. That, plus the friendships I made, the memories I have and the experiences are plenty. The rest: lanyards and program books, school projects and employee handbooks, software manuals, broken plaques, and coffee mugs were dumped. I moved on and it felt great!"

Purging-By-Output

Recently a client told me, "I have hundreds of photos. I just don't have any pictures!" Sometimes enjoying what you've inputted is best achieved by outputting it. So print out an exceptional photograph and frame it. You might even find that you can get rid of something once it's outputted. For instance, my client has a large stack of professional reading. He asked me "What's the best way to organize my professsional reading?" "Read it," I replied. "Turn it into knowledge."

I know that's easier than it sounds but an oft overlooked method for making endless information go away is to turn it into something, to produce something with it. The information you may be inputting into your life might well have an even better output. My client Doug turned tons of notes, documents, and files accumulated during his career in public health into a best-selling book.

Scrapbooking is a time-honored way of moving mere information into a meaningful output. Create a new spin with a digital album. Perhaps the information you accumulate would make great blog content, a good ebook, or a smashing adult education class. If you're crafty, books can be turned into furniture and magazines can be turned into jewelry. For more ideas visit www.squidoo.com/paper-beads and the WebEcoist website (www.tinyurl.com/86gmbda).

Purging Exercise

Purging takes practice. George Carlin said, "Isn't it a bit unnerving that doctors call what they do *practice?*" It's also a little unnerving to cultivate new organizing skills, but new times demand it. Here's an exercise to develop your purging skills. It graduates you from easy purging to more difficult purging.

1. Open up your Favorites/Bookmarks drop down list.

2. Delete 25% from the list. Start with the ones you don't recognize at all. Move to the ones that you're sure you no longer need.

3. Wait one week and go back to the list and delete one out of every ten (10% more).

4. Move onto your RSS feeds. Delete 25% of them.

5. Wait one week and go back and delete one out of every ten (10% more).

6. Move on to digital photos. Delete one out of every ten (10% of them).

7. If you're really up to the challenge, purge some of the books on your bookshelves.

8. A tough challenge for some women is getting rid of shoes. If you can purge books and shoes, you're at the top of the purging class!

Information Afterlife

Information is endless and time is not. The most unusual expression of this is that information actually lives on after you die. (Google remembers your searches forever.) Information afterlife is peculiar to the Era of Endless and, unfortunately, yet another aspect of getting information organized. My client's sister, Maxine, died suddenly. Eventually it came time to settle Maxine's estate. Nobody in the family knew the passwords to her bank accounts, retirement accounts, or investments. Even if they did, only five states as of the printing of this book (Idaho, Indiana, Oklahoma, Rhode Island and Connecticut) have passed laws granting a designated personal representative control of the deceased's digital assets.

Examples of digital assets are:

- email
- social media accounts
- digital collections
- online bank, investment and retirement accounts
- domain names
- online subscriptions
- frequent flyer miles
- blog content
- websites
- and even your video game avatars!

Your user codes and passwords will be necessary to unlock these digital assets from your computer hard drive, external flash drives, CDs and web or cloud-based portals.

Estate laws, end-of-life planning, terms of service agreements, documents providing for powers of attorney in the event of your death or incapacitation—all these legal matters and more have not kept pace with digital society. Maxine's family spent many hours and a lot of money for attorneys to settle her estate with the courts. To prevent your family from being locked out, quite literally, of your digital assets:

Create a Digital Estate Plan

Designate a digital assets representative. This may or may not be the same person as your executor. It should be someone you trust who is digitally-savvy.

Print out on good old-fashioned hard copy paper, your passwords, user codes, answers to security questions, and other access information. Be certain this document accompanies your Will but is not in the Will itself. This will allow you to easily change access information without having to alter the Will itself. Also, since Wills become public records, you don't want any access information to be disclosed publicly.

- Keep an electronic and/or web version of your passwords, user codes, and answers to security questions in a password-protected file. Send a copy to your representative along with the password to access it.
- Include a list of your account numbers and the names of the financial institutions with automatic payments, deposits, transfers, debits, and other automated financial transactions you have established. Leave your representative explicit instructions on your wishes to cancel, modify, or maintain automated transactions.
- Make a list of all your social media accounts. Most people request they be closed and taken down to prevent undue demands on your family to maintain them, the possibility of hacking or identity theft, and to facilitate emotional closure. If you and your family feel differently, leave explicit instructions about your preferences.
- Identify beneficiaries of any of your digital assets. For instance, if you want to pass your digital collection of old movies, digital genealogy records, or digital photographs onto specific relatives, explicitly state that in your Will.
- Check out a service like www.deleteme.com if you want to take steps now to lower your digital profile so there is less information to contend with after your demise.

What Is Worth Passing On?

In the Era of Endless, even one individual can accumulate a substantial amount of information in a lifetime. The list, while not endless, is certainly long and can include hardcopy or digital letters, diaries, photos, memoirs, scrapbooks, photo albums, professional papers, genealogy information, speeches, business records, legal documents, minutes, health records, financial information, files, brochures, flyers, posters, videos, audio tapes, artifacts, art, books, maps, music, blogs, email, websites, etc., etc., etc....

Not all of this information is worthy of passing along to the next generation who will be burdened to identify, organize, sort, appraise, store, maintain, preserve, and otherwise process it if you do not do this now while you are in good health.

Of equal concern is leaving too little. "We're not talking here about institutional archives or the records of your everyday life but about family archives. These memories speak to the soul of your family," Melissa Mannon, a professional archivist said in a recent interview. Archivists fear that valuable family, community, and cultural memories will be lost because people do not know how to save all the various formats that information now embodies. Valuable information can be lost due to computer hacking and other mischief. Cloud security can be breached. Web companies go under.

If the soul of your family resides even partially inside the information you have:

- Take the time to create your family's special collection.
- Safeguard it by backing it up in more than one location.
- Create an index to the collection of what is where and how to access it.
- Read the book, *The Unofficial Family Archivist* for more instructions.

---

[1] Linda Stone, "Continuous Partial Attention," Businessweek.com, 2008

[2] *Delete,* pg. 171

[3] Tim Ferris, "12 Filtering Tips for Better Information in Half the Time," fourhourworkweek blog, 2007

ERA OF ENDLESS
PART FOUR

WHAT TO DO WHEN INTERRUPTION IS ENDLESS AND TIME IS NOT

TAKE A FRESH LOOK AT
THE POSITIVE SIDE OF INTERRUPTION

In an episode of *Roseanne*, the 70s TV sitcom, Roseanne Barr plays a waitress in a diner. After a hard day at work she goes home. At the dinner table, Roseanne complains to her family about this guy who came into the diner, demanded food, paid her with barely a tip and had a bad attitude. She called him a low-life. Her daughter exclaimed, "Mom, that wasn't a low-life; that was a customer!"

Just like Roseanne, who has yet to learn that customers—even grouchy ones—are her job, we have to learn that interruptions are a permanent part of the Era of Endless. That doesn't mean disruptive elements should rule the day; it does mean that the notion of interruption in the Era of Endless is evolving and you can evolve with it. Try to see interruptions through the eyes of digital natives weaned on computers and social media. What you might understand as interruptions and distractions are to them digital messages that carry potential, opportunity and possibility—what I call POP.

Potential

- Potentially, a tweet, a text, or other digital message can give you an avenue to participate in real-time conversations and events that you otherwise might not have been able to join.
- You could potentially change an appointment, set up a meeting, or organize an event faster and easier than through other methods.
- Receiving a digital message has the potential to introduce you to something immediately relevant or useful.

Opportunity

- Digital messages can provide an instant opportunity for you to be notified of a mistake and correct it on the spot.
- You can receive and provide feedback when there might be no other opportunity.

- The opportunity to share information in the moment enhances its impact.
- Learning, seeing, and knowing something new in real-time or close-time can be an opportunity for great joy.

Possibility

- Digital messages make it possible for you to keep up with what's new while it's happening.
- Real-time information could possibly allow you to avert a crisis, permit you to alter a plan, or give you the chance to change course.
- Receiving and transmitting messages in diverse formats can improve interaction and bring in voices not typically heard.

Hopefully, I've convinced you that there is a positive side to interruptions. They're not the enemy of time management. Recent surveys reveal that 32% of people under the age of 25 don't mind an interruption while eating and 24% see no problem taking a call or text while on the toilet.[1] Those of us over 25 tend to draw the line in the sand a little further out. In the Era of Endless, the most effective solutions for coping with interruptions, distractions, and temptations are those that try to strike a balance between embracing them and avoiding their excesses. In that spirit, here is what I have to offer.

Context Counts

In the Era of Endless interruptions you still have to make an effort to control the excesses. It starts with context. Context means taking into account what you're already doing when the interruption arrived. The machines are dumb. Your smartphone, tablet, and computer don't know the importance of your current task. They don't know if what you're doing now is worth putting aside, even for just a moment, in order to respond to the interruption. Only you can assess that. Forget about approaching the issue of interruptions from the point of view of their *content* and consider instead the *context* of what you're currently doing as the point of departure for entertaining interruptions.

- If your current task or project is time-sensitive, you may need to consider ignoring all but the most urgent interruptions.
- If what you are doing is on someone else's critical path or is holding up their work, be more discerning about entertaining interruptions.
- If the context of what you are doing is complex or involves a highly focused learning curve, that's a limited-interruption scenario.
- If dividing your attention is hazardous or dangerous, don't allow interruptions. In 2010, at least 3,092 people were killed in distraction-related car crashes, accounting for approximately one in every ten fatalities on the nation's roadways.[2] Emergency rooms report a spike in people walking into poles, falling down manholes, and crashing into each other while texting and walking on busy city streets.
- If what you're currently doing clears the deck for the rest of the day, makes you feel in control, or lowers your stress, it might be worth your while to protect it from distraction and interruption. When you accomplish something early in the day before you open the flood-gates of interruptions, you could experience a sense of meaning and accomplishment that can last the entire day.

It is well-documented that undistracted time is necessary for excellence. In her book, *Quiet: The Power of Introverts in a World That Can't Stop Talking,* author Susan Cain summarizes study upon study about musicians, chess players, and athletes who claim that intense, singular concentration is what it takes to be excellent. People, no matter how supportive they are—including teammates, coaches, and teachers—can be a distraction. Top performers in companies, from sales to computer programmers, do their best when given privacy, personal space, and freedom from interruption.[3]

Take the Wrapper Off the Transporter

Responding to what seems like urgency is one way interruptions can get the better of us. Urgency can be seductive. Every time a vibrantly colorful graphic announcing "Breaking News" in big letters (accompanied by an engaging soundtrack and a passionate voice-over) displays on my TV I am certain something new and urgent is happening in the world. But "breaking news" often turns out to be a rehash of a prior broadcast with nothing new or urgent at all. Still, it gets my attention every time. The actual ding of a teasing text message morsel can start the brain anticipating new, unpredictable information much like the mouth salivating at the sight of yummy food.[4] Beware of the urgency wrapper of digital messages. Just because it dings, rings, flashes, or vibrates and has the capacity to find you wherever you are, that doesn't mean the message or content is crucial.

Different Work in Different Environments

Different kinds of work require different levels of focus. I once took an informal poll of people hunched over their computer working solo at Starbucks. After profusely apologizing for interrupting them, I learned that most were looking for just enough background noise to make them feel in good company, but not so much that they were distracted from their work.

Strategic planning, brainstorming, creative projects, and large group work thrives in open spaces with lots of light and windows and plenty of space to spread out. Loud talk, patching in people via Skype, and lots of input which might otherwise be considered interruptive are welcome in this scenario.

At the opposite end of the spectrum is intense, solitary work such as analysis and writing. These are best accomplished in smaller, quiet spaces, such as study cubbies at the library where you turn off your cell phone and interruptions are held to a minimum. A client of mine does her professional reading in the lobby of a local hospital across the street from her office. "That's where I hide," she tells me. Another client checks into a hotel for two days to do her taxes. "Only my family knows how to reach me. After working a few hours, I can take a swim, workout in the gym, or get a massage. Meals are convenient and the whole idea of a dedicated place seems to make me more productive."

When choosing the best place for working on a task, ask yourself the questions:

- What is the task-at-hand?
- What level of focus does the task require?
- Intense, solitary work?
- Wide-ranging, large group work?
- Purposeful, small group work?
- What setting would best support the task?

Don't Set Yourself Up

"The tablet with its Internet, email, ebooks, YouTube, iPod, iTunes, and access to 90,000 apps was a bit too much for me," my client confessed. "I needed to read online newspapers and write a blog. But when I hunkered down to work at a local coffee shop, I watched a short film, bought a book, checked out Facebook, and downloaded an app that monitors my prescriptions for drug interactions. All cool, but the blog took me probably twice as long to write. Now when I blog, I take my Netbook with me and leave the tablet at home."

Another client plans her parties and organizers her travels at home, sitting in front of a good, old PC. "Even though I have an iPad and a tablet, I just know I can't get that kind of work done unless I am away from all the goodies on my iPad," she confesses. You're a grown person and probably know by now which digital distractions and temptations you are most vulnerable to. Consider the kind of work you have to do and give thought to the best device to use and the environment in which to do it.

Reconsider Instant Messaging

According to the latest statistical report from Radicati Group, Inc., the typical corporate email user sends and receives 105 email messages per day.[5] Email seems to reduce a special kind of interruption: people who come unannounced into other people's offices. But instant messaging (IM) is making a comeback as a better choice to reduce interruptions. Some people may say that IM is as disruptive as phone calls and emails, but a joint study by Ohio State University and the

University of California, Irvine, challenges that notion. Researchers found that workers using instant messaging report fewer interruptions than their colleagues who do not use instant messaging[6]. IM was proven to actually substitute for face-to-face conversation, emails, and phone calls, cutting down more intrusive interruptions. Not only is the communication brief and to the point, but dismissing or delaying a response with IM is socially and professionally acceptable.

Working Memory Prostheses

Working memory is like a scratch pad or sticky note in your head. You can hold up to four pieces of information in mind at any one time. Four grocery items, four errands to run, the names of four people, etc. When you're interrupted, bam! The list can go out the window, figuratively speaking.

Dr. Clifford Nass, a researcher at Stanford, explored the theory that people who heavily multitask will develop strong working memories. But his research shows just the opposite. Memory for holding information in mind, filtering information, and switching between tasks is no better with multi-taskers than single-taskers.[7] In the Era of Endless interruption, one defense might be training exercises for the brain that improve working memory. There is little doubt these exercises can be helpful under controlled conditions with professional trainers but there is controversy about usage by the general public.[8] Until home games and exercises for improving working memory become more reliable and affordable, working memory prosthetics is the way to go. They are:

Lists and more lists. Humans have spent millions of years being list-makers, and for good reason. Getting things out of your head gives your working memory a break. If a task or project is complex—it has more than two steps—make a list. The more moving parts there are to a task, the more you need to make a list. Even full-blown project management methods begin with specifying a list of tasks.

Write out instructions and directions unless they are an ingrained habit or very routine. Why tax your working memory when you can use a cheat sheet?

Use artifacts. If you have difficulty holding in mind where you left off when you got interrupted use tangible reminders, called artifacts. For instance, I advise my clients to bring an artifact with them when they leave a room. An unopened envelope as a reminder you were opening the mail. A washcloth to remind you were folding laundry. Even a Post-it note with nothing written on it can remind you to go back to the computer. Grab something tangible that you can feel in your hand.

Write on your hand. No. I'm only kidding. When I encounter an adult who writes on their hand, I know instantly that they have a weak working memory. Perhaps they have ADD or another disorder that affects their executive function or maybe the Era of Endless interruptions has just gotten the best of them. Write on your hand if you must, but here are other choices.

- **Write on tangible sticky notes** and leave them in a prominent place.

- **Use digital sticky notes.** I like to use the versatile, colorful, scalable, movable sticky notes—and even alarms—from the website www.zhornsoftware.co.uk/stickies/

- **Make a quick recorded message.** Instacorder is an iPhone app that allows you to push the record button and record a voice memo. When you release the button, the message is sent to you via email.

- **Snap a fast photo** with your smartphone showing you where you left off.

- **Leave a message** to yourself on your voicemail.

Reduce Distractions

Your working memory is competing against many other inputs to hold on to the information you want it to cling to: loud kids, ringing phones, inc-oming texts, outgoing faxes, internal worries (Do I have gas in the car? Did I give the kids lunch money? Is my lipstick on?), visual distractions like a full inbox, and on and on. Give your working memory a fighting chance. Reduce distractions, keep your desk uncluttered, your filters up, and control as many distractions as you can. One of my clients who works from home displays a sign on her home office door that says, "Don't Even Think About It." Short of an emergency, her kids know not to disturb her. On the other hand, every two hours, she comes out of the office and gives her full attention to the kids for half an hour.

My next door neighbor took me for a drive in her brand new 2013 vehicle. The dashboard was part cockpit and part tablet touchscreen. Engineers claim that the audio-enabled technologies of Bluetooth, voice command, voice recognition, and streaming audio are no more distracting than the radio and CD player on "older" vehicles. And that may be true. We do not yet have enough data to make any conclusions about the effect of these features on driver distraction. Waiting in the wings are dashboard features that go beyond touchscreen to finger swipe, contacts and calendar entries, drag and drop, multiple social media feeds, and 3-D visual effects that can compete with the most sophisticated indoor entertainment centers. We'll need to be vigilant about protecting our driving.

Another area to protect is sleep. Tweens are waking in the middle of the night to check Facebook and Twitter. Some are sleeping with their devices under their pillows. This is not like in past eras when we were young and pulled the covers over our heads and read by flashlight till our parents caught us. The stimulation of online games, texting, and videos is way more disruptive for sleep than even the wildest imagination ignited by a great book. According to the National Sleep Foundation, *lights out* means that everything with a screen should be off-limits at least a half hour before bedtime. Spend that time reading a book, soaking in a hot tub, or otherwise winding down from endlessness.

[1] William Klemm, PhD, "Training Working Memory," *Psychology Today*, March 2012

[2] Retrevo.com, survey results, 2011

[3] Susan Cain, *Quiet: The Power of Introverts in a World That Can't Stop Talking,* pgs. 81-84

[4] Kent C. Berridge and Terry E. Robinson, "What is the Role of Dopamine in Reward," Brain Research Reviews, 1998

[5] Radicati Group, Inc., Email Statistics Report, 2011-2015

[6] Ohio State University. *"Instant Messaging Proves Useful in Reducing Workplace Interruption,"* 2008

[7] Dr. Clifford Nass, "Multitasking: Effects on You and Your Children," YouTube video, November, 2012

ERA OF ENDLESS

PART FIVE

WHAT TO DO WHEN
WORK IS ENDLESS
AND TIME IS NOT

WORK IN THE ERA OF ENDLESS

Of course, you don't work endlessly. You're not a beast of burden. In the Era of Endless, endless work means that even though you are personally more productive, your productivity is not generating a leisure dividend. In the past, productivity won people more leisure time, not without a fight, of course, but people also enjoyed the fruits of their labor, one of which was leisure. The more productive you were, the more leisure you had.

In the Era of Endless instead of reinvesting our productivity gains into leisure, we reinvest it into more work. Sometimes we do this for job security, especially as Americans struggle to come out of a deep and enduring recession. People are concerned that if they don't keep working, their boss will replace them. 50% of respondents to a recent Verizon survey state, "My job security depends on the boss seeing me connected," meaning on the phone, the computer, or the Internet even during lunch and other times *once reserved for non-work.* 15% of us plan on attending a work-related phone call or web meeting on our next vacation.[1]

It's so easy to keep working. One more work-related email is like brain candy, instant gratification. You can do it with maximum effect and minimal effort and that's why it's so enticing. Working via digital connectedness during times reserved for non-work is the source of *work creep.* In the Era of Endless, work creep not only extends your working time, but it also intrudes into your personal time. Like the Energizer bunny, you keep going and going until the line between work and leisure becomes more and more blurry.

Surprisingly, more than two-thirds of all health-related productivity losses are not due to people missing work. According to a study in the *Journal of Occupational and Environmental Medicine,* productivity loss is the result of employees with chronic or contagious ailments who still show up for work and perform poorly. Even depression, once associated with stressful work, is now more commonly the result of overtime. The more hours worked above eight hours a day, the more depression there is.[2] You, and millions of others, are working through meals, through illness, through family dinners, and baseball games. You may not be a beast of burden, but it can sure feel that way when work is endless and time is not.

Personal Productivity

Personal productivity is difficult to measure. When you get something done in less time it's not like you can bank the savings, but the signs of productivity are everywhere. If you traded up from the cell phone to a smartphone, you're more productive because you have the Internet in your pocket. If you use GPS instead of a map, you're more productive. I sell books at conferences and swipe the purchasers' credit cards on my smartphone which is **wwwaaaayyyy** more productive than taking checks or using a credit card machine. Snapping a picture of your check and depositing it directly from your iPhone is more productive than standing in line at the bank. Using an app to find the least expensive merchandise without scouting the Internet or the mall, or taking a blood pressure reading and sending it to your doctor via email; these are just a few of the hundreds of ways each day you are more productive than last year, last month, or even yesterday.

As of the printing of this book, there were 775,000 apps, most designed in one way or another to help you get something done in less time. So, though you can't deposit the time saved from personal productivity, it's safe to say you deserve to cash in on your leisure dividend. Think of it this way. Leisure is an expression of self-worth. By taking personal time you have earned by being productive and working smarter not harder, you express your self-worth—and provide for your self-preservation!

Cash In On Your Leisure Dividend

Take Time to Eat. In her book, *How Did I Get So Busy,* Valorie Burton notes that 58% of Americans admit to skipping lunch, many substituting with high-caffeine drinks and sugar-loaded energy bars. I would venture to guess that your personal productivity dividend is big enough to take a full hour for lunch. Every organ in your body will thank you, not only in the short-run with mental clarity and physical energy, but also in the long-run with lowered risk for heart disease, better digestion, and stronger lungs.

Take Your Vacation Days. A 2012 survey by Expedia reports that 37% of US employees cancelled a portion of their vacation because of work. Scientists have found that it takes at least three days to relax and actually feel you're on vacation. Stick three days before or after a weekend and go on a vacation.

Provide Great Coverage. I recognize that taking time away from work is easier said than done. If you provide great coverage for those maintaining your job while you're gone, you'll find taking time off is less stressful and you'll be less apt to cancel it.

- Make written instructions to co-workers, temps, or babysitters about how to hold down the fort in your absence.
- Leave YouTube videos, photographs, or other visual aids that show others how to cover your work while you're away.
- Stay connected to co-workers, babysitters, or anyone else covering for you via Skype or FaceTime without breaking your vacation.
- Plan time in your schedule to adequately wrap up loose ends before leaving.

Own Your Personal Days. You work hard. You work smart. And you work long. Your leisure dividend includes using 50% of your personal days for time out (assuming you are employed and you even *have* them!) I know personal days are reserved for really urgent situations that you can't predict, but I think you should *predict* using half of them and reserve the other half for emergencies. It's really not so hard to predict when you might need a personal day. Here are some situations my clients recommend:

- The day after a very long, difficult project.
- The day school starts if you have little ones.
- April 10th to give you a boost for working on taxes.
- A day between Christmas and New Year.

- Your birthday.
- The day after any day you already know will be stressful or a logistical nightmare.

Unplanned Weekends. Plan nothing one Saturday per month and one Sunday per month but not on the same weekend. By *plan nothing*, I mean keep it unscheduled and uncommitted. Use it to do what you find yourself in the mood to do even if it's being lazy, doing something spontaneous, or working. The point is not necessarily engaging in leisure as much as letting your mood rather than your schedule drive the day.

Digital Leisure

When work is virtually endless and time is not, you need to find leisure where you can. Digital leisure has many benefits. Breaking from work to "snack" on email—Angry Birds, tweets, blogs, or Facebook—can be just plain fun, as well as offering these benefits:

- Alleviates fatigue.
- Becomes a rhythm or pacing that increases productivity.
- Offers an opportunity to mentally noodle on something while you are doing something else.
- Incubates ideas.
- Is a problem-solving strategy.
- Improves creativity.
- Breaks you out of ruts and routines.

Non-Digital Leisure

As a digital immigrant, I might be biased, but I believe non-digital leisure is superior to digital leisure for deeper relaxation and restorative, recreative benefits. Many educators, medical doctors, and pediatricians agree. The two most important benefits of non-digital leisure over digital leisure are that non-digital leisure provides: 1) the **physical** opportunity to be away from devices, machines and screens allowing you to move and stretch, and 2) a substantial **mental break** away from devices, machines and screens.

Non-Digital Leisure is best achieved when it:

- Involves motion such as stretching, walking, dancing, or climbing.
- Is not necessarily goal-oriented.
- Is unmediated by devices, machines, or screens.
- Fully engages your undivided attention to a singular activity.

Spending time in nature (or even viewing it) has been shown in numerous studies to alter your physical and emotional response to stress. A review of 120 studies published in 2009 by the *International Journal of Public Health* found that time spent in parks, gardens, waterfronts, forests, or wilderness settings was associated with a more positive attitude, lower pulse rate and other markers of well-being.

7 Non-Digital Leisure Activities

- Napping. In Japan, companies allow you to take naps on the job in special napping rooms. If you nap on a park bench in Japan, the cops leave you alone!
- Family dinners.
- Socializing with friends.
- Physical exercise of any kind, but especially walking.
- Real-time dating.
- Sex with a live person.
- Sleep.

A recent edition of the *Wall Street Journal* reported on the growing trend that people use their beds as their offices. They prop up, get comfy with their devices, and search the web, check email, or post to Facebook. The same week, the National Sleep Foundation reported that 63% of people say their sleeping needs are unmet during the week. It doesn't take a rocket scientist to make a connection. Of course, all sleep deprivation is not due to using devices in bed, but the research is conclusive that such activities do not foster, and often undermine, adequate sleep, especially in young adults.

Here's what happens: Cortisol and adrenaline, two of the body's natural stimulants, are released during video games, movies, and online gambling, and to a lesser extent with email, web surfing, and Facebook. The light from the screen can send disruptive signals to the brain telling it to wake up rather than power down. According to Gary Small, M.D., the author of *iBrain*, 80% of students responding to a survey, said they **never** get a good night's sleep during the week. Many sleep with their phones on vibrate like some kind of freaking emergency room doctor![3] Children are quick to mimic your example of working in bed. Sleep needs and sleeping cycles of children are more susceptible to the kind of disruption that devices cause. For that reason alone, consider only non-digital activities in the sack.

Let's face it. You can't always plan a vacation when it's most needed, but there are times when a brief break will have to do. Take a real break—a Green Break. A Green Break provides the most basic elements of a vacation in brief, miniature form.

Take a Green Break

1. Get a glass of water.
2. Go outdoors. Any place with nature will do—a tree, shrub, bush, hedge, or flower.
3. Stand in front of the object of nature.
4. Focus your eyes on it for the slow count of 10.
5. As you count to 10 breathe in and sweep your arms up over your head till your hands touch.
6. Let your breath out and lower your arms to your sides as you count to 10.
7. Repeat this three times. Do it slowly and let your breath in and out fully
8. Drink some water.
9. Repeat another two times, more if you like (and if you aren't dizzy!) The oxygen to the brain clears brain fog. Drinking water provides hydration. And the oxygen and hydration work together to counteract stress.

Getting Organized in the Era of Endless

Combine Digital and Non-Digital Leisure

When work is endless and time is not, a mix of digital and non-digital leisure is in order. My client, Emily, is a good example. Emily and her 13 and 15 year old daughters go camping regularly. "The point is to get the girls out into nature," Emily says. "We try to leave most of our tech toys at home." But Emily is realistic. The ability to use GPS, make calls in an emergency, or hunker down in the tent during a rainstorm with a good video or ebook can be a real asset. "I allow the girls to mix in a little bit of their kind of entertainment as long as they also get a good portion of stars and clouds, fresh air and trees," Emily maintains. It's all about balance. A poison plant app works well in the woods.

The average American teenager sends or receives 75 text messages a day. "Since luxury, as any economist will tell you, is a function of scarcity, the children of tomorrow…will crave nothing more than freedom, if only for a short while, from all the blinking machines, streaming videos and scrolling headlines that leave them feeling empty and too full all at once."[4] Nature is one of those forms of freedom.

What To Do About Work Creep

In the Era of Endless, an argument could be made that whatever productivity gains we accrue might well be lost to work creep. To combat work creep:

Adjust Expectations

My teenaged niece told me that the dating game has changed. It used to be that if you responded to a perspective date sooner than two days, you looked desperate. Now if you don't return a call, text, or email to an online prospective date within hours, you're considered not interested. In the business world, nearly 75% of our co-workers expect us to respond to emails within four hours or less, according to a recent survey conducted by Toister Performance Solutions, Inc. Almost 25% of respondents are particularly impatient, saying they expect co-workers to respond to emails within one hour. I don't know about the dating world, but in the world of business, if you continually respond within minutes, that's what recipients will expect of you. And you'll internalize that expectation of yourself causing extra stress. Adjust people's expectations by being less reactive about emailing. With few exceptions, one day is still an acceptable protocol to anything other than the most important or urgent messages.

Personal and Family Technology Policy

The way you respond to work creep sends a strong message to your kids about the sanctity (or lack thereof) of family time. Consider developing a simple personal and family policy. The more you draw the line on work, the more the next generation will get the message. Here's a sample I helped develop with one of my clients. Every family is different but the more the rules apply to everyone—parents and children—the better.

- No devices at the dinner table. All devices are treated equally whether it's an iPad, TV, tablet, iPhone, or anything that beeps, rings, or flashes.
- No screens of any kind after 9 p.m.
- No phones within 10 feet of water whether it's the ocean, a pool, the bathtub, or the toilet.
- No texting in front of grandma.
- No driver in this family will ever text while driving.
- Hugs, eye contact, and live conversation will dominate in this family over texts, calls, and technology.
- If the sun and school are out, you will find us outdoors.

In the ping of a text or a few seconds of a ringtone as you focus on your device, your child can fall from the monkey bars or make a soccer goal you might miss. Your loved one's body language could be saying "I need a friend," and you could miss it. Your spouse's touch or smile might go unnoticed. There are moments that cannot be replaced by work, productivity, or efficiency. Create customized personal and family policies that keep your quality of life priorities well in front of endless connectedness and the stress of work creep.

Delegate To The Machines

I know it sounds like a contradiction. I've been advocating for more face-time and less devices. But in the Era of Endless work, one way to generate more leisure is to be certain that you are delegating everything you possibly can to the machines. A recent *Wired Magazine* article profiled an inventor, Dominic Wilcox. Wilcox rightly observes that it's too much work to get lost when you're traveling to any destination: too much anxiety, mental energy, emotion, logistics, being late, stress, and so forth. He invented shoes with a GPS in them. You upload your required destination to the shoes and a GPS device embedded in the heel activates with a heel click just like Dorothy in the Wizard of Oz. A ring of LED lights shine in the correct direction, leading the way. Follow the yellow brick road.

Well, okay, maybe you don't want to go that far, but there are some functions you can ***delegate*** to machines. You can fully ***participate*** in modernity, ***make*** the best ***use of*** technology, AND ***directly reduce your workload if you have:***

- A web-based file storage for notes, random thoughts, ideas, lists, and bits of information. Try Evernote.
- A secure place for passwords and other sensitive information. Try LastPass, KeePass, or 1Password.
- Secure, online banking and auto bill pay. See your bank's website.
- The capacity to have your smartphone tracked in the event of theft or loss. Check out Plan B, an app on Google Play for Androids, and Find My Phone at the App Store.
- A shopping scanner. Check out www.tinyurl.com/bgxczao, the pcmag website.
- A productivity tool that combines tasks with your calendar/schedule. Check out Coolendar, Reqall, and 1Calendar.
- A way to transcribe voicemail to text. Try YouMail.

- A way to convert text to voice, from the makeuseof website. www.tinyurl.com/a9r6lzw
- Cloud storage for your files. Try www.dropbox.com.

You can delegate a lot of tasks to the machines using apps. Read this article (www.tinyurl.com/abl3fm9) on apps that will maximize your effect and minimize your effort.

Practice Triage

When work is endless and time is not, triage might be a good solution, especially if you've unsuccessfully tried tactics carried over from other eras for task and time management, like urgent and important matrixes or hierarchical decision-trees. In the Era of Endless work, you need to step up from prioritizing to triaging.

Triage is like prioritizing on steroids. I'm certainly no expert when it comes to disaster preparedness, but I'm certified in Community Emergency Response Team (www.cert.org), a civilian training program. We learn that if adequate resources are available, you try to save everyone. But triage is a process used to quickly sort injured people into groups based on their likely benefit from immediate care *when resources are scarce or limited.* Triage assumes you do not have enough resources on the disaster scene (like medical supplies, first-responders, personnel, and equipment) to treat everyone.

Even patients who come through a hospital emergency room aren't treated on a first-come, first-serve basis. Doctors don't attend to the people who scream the loudest. A triage nurse quickly assesses who needs urgent care and who can wait because there's never enough time or resources to treat everyone at the same time.

In the Era of Endless, triaging (rather than simply prioritizing) seems more appropriate for tasks and work that flies into our radar or endlessly creep in from many places. Instead of a shortage of medical resources, in the Era of Endless *time* is the non-renewable, limited resource. Rather than working endlessly and treating all tasks, projects, and inputs equally, triage them.

A term used in disaster preparedness is "walking wounded"— those who will likely survive their injuries without immediate care.

That's good. That means precious re-sources can be devoted to others in more urgent need. Scrutinize your tasks and To-Dos. Are there tasks that can survive without you? In other words, is there stuff you don't really need to be doing? Delegate to the machines (or other people) the tasks that can survive without your help. Other strategies are rescheduling or canceling those non-urgent tasks. When you delegate, reschedule, or cancel the tasks that can get done without you, the limited resource of your time can be devoted to priority tasks that do require your attention.

Disaster victims in need of complex medical attention beyond the resources of personnel on the scene are triaged by moving them to a special designated place or tagging them in some way that indicates their need for additional attention and care. Stop the bleeding first and open the airways, we disaster preparedness folks are told, until more medical help arrives. In organizing terms, stopping the bleeding and opening up the airways means doing the most effective thing possible in the time available to you. You won't be able to complete a complex project all at once, but there's always something you can do to be effective. That might mean initiating a meeting, developing an action plan, holding a brainstorming session, or doing something as simple as sending a well-crafted email or making a concise phone call.

People who triage well do it quickly on their feet, often based on their emotions and intuition. First-responders to a disaster scene simply *know* how to allocate their resources for maximum effect for the greatest number of people. David Allen, the productivity expert, advises:

> "Prioritize according to energy, mood, intuition, and emotion. Learn to listen to and trust your heart. Or your intuition, or your gut or the seat of your pants or whatever anatomy is the source of that mysteriously wonderful 'still, small voice' that somehow knows you better than you do, and knows what is better for you than you do. LISTEN to it...take the risk to move on your best guess, pay attention to the results and course-correct as you keep moving along."[5]

Some tasks are clarified by a hard deadline or a set-in-concrete due date leaving little wiggle room for prioritizing. But much of what we do in the Era of Endless is really a judgment call. If it *feels* important for you, it probably is. Video blogger, Ze Frank suggests making a list of all the things you need to do and then reading it out loud to yourself. If it *sounds* important as you read it, there's a good chance you've made the right call.

What if you don't have the instincts of a first-responder to prioritize, re-prioritize, and triage your tasks and To-Dos as you go along? I'd like to make some recommendations based on more than two decades of organizing thousands of clients.

Triage Tips

- **Alleviate worry.** "I make a careful To-Do list. I prioritize it every day. I assign A, B, and C to each task and integrate new tasks as soon as I learn of them. Then, when I wake up the morning I do one or two tasks that immediately alleviates worry whether they're on my list or not," a client tells me. Dispelling worry is a great use of your time. It clears the head and frees you from emotional drains that will thwart all your other work.

- **Alleviate guilt.** Like assuaging worry, doing tasks that free you from guilt will allow you to focus on other work.

- **Get someone off your back.** This definitely counts as a justifiable way to triage which tasks to do first.

- **Break the tie.** In the Era of Endless work, priorities compete. You have to find some way to break the tie, otherwise your work will get stalled in indecision. Make a judgment call, use your intuition, do the one you like the best, do the one that is the most difficult, do the one that is the easiest. It doesn't matter. Just break the tie. If two priorities are truly tied, then the consequences of choosing one over the other will be relatively equal. It will be just as well to do one or just as well to do the other. The closer the priorities are, the closer the consequences are. Doing either is a good choice. Trying to endlessly figure out which is best to do, is not a good use of your time.

- **Choose the option** that makes or saves the company money. The bottom line is always a good clue for where to spend your time.

Traditional time management schemes from previous eras tend to underestimate the need for triaging tasks as we go along. Francis Wade has developed a time management program he calls Time Management 2.0 that provides for the capture and triage of time demands coming in from multiple directions. Take a look at www.2time-sys.com

Saying No: An Organizational Classic

Part of quality of life is following through on your commitments, being reliable and trustworthy in your obligations to others (and to yourself), and being someone that other people can count on to do what you promise to do. If you don't form commitments you'll likely get none in return. If you're obligated to nobody but yourself, you'll live a pretty lonely life. In the Era of Endless, commitments that over-extend us begin to feel like work even if they didn't start out that way.

Without overdoing the disaster preparedness analogy, I want to borrow another concept from that field to use in the Era of Endless work. It's the idea of prevention.

We can learn what to do when we catch on fire, get hit by lightning, or fall through the ice, but nothing maximizes your effect and minimizes your effort better than not getting into these situations in the first place. In the Era of Endless work, preventing over-commitment takes the form of saying *No*. It's such a little word, even smaller than Yes, but it can actually be harder to say. Yes is cleaner. It needs no explanation, carries no guilt, and is downright friendly. *No* can seem rejecting or uncooperative and often requires explanation.

Saying *No* without using the word is a classic organizing tip, maybe even more appropriate to the Era of Endless than in previous eras. We tend to pile-on commitments and obligations at work, home, community, school, and in the volunteer arena. Maybe we think we're so productive, we can absorb more and more things to do. Or perhaps we just fail to ask ourselves, "Am I really committed to this commitment?" You won't always be able to feel good about your commitments and obligations. Some will be burdensome and feel like work no matter what. But with a little prevention you'll have the satisfaction of knowing you intentionally signed-up rather than defaulted to *Yes* when you could have said *No*.

Three Powerful Ways to Say No Without Uttering the Word

1. Find a declination phrase that is comfortable to you. It's important to acknowledge that you've been asked to commit to something. Take it as a compliment to your productivity or skills. And decline it, without saying *No*. Find a phrase that works for you. I teach my clients to say: "Thanks for asking me but I can't do that job justice right now." This phrase acknowledges the asker, takes the request seriously, and declines gracefully. Here's another phrase a client taught me: "If you still need help two months from now, contact me."

2. Learn a little negotiation. Here's an example of negotiating the timetable at work:

Getting Organized in the Era of Endless

If you can't negotiate the timetable, try negotiating the scope of work:

Or,

A good resource for learning the basics of negotiation is the book *Negotiation for Dummies*.

3. Deliver an Impact Statement. Instead of saying *No* you say Yes but make it clear that there is an impact or consequence.

The Law of Diminishing Returns

In the Era of Endless work it's easy to break the Law of Diminishing Returns. It's not like you'll get arrested or anything. The Law of Diminishing Returns is actually an economic law very appropriate to the Era of Endless work. It's defined as "The tendency for a continuing effort toward a particular goal to decline in effectiveness after a certain level of result has been achieved."

Let me give you an example. My client Ann is an assistant human resources director for a large law firm. Her job is to recruit qualified prospective attorneys to work for the firm. She reads resumes, goes to college job fairs, addresses law associations, networks, networks, and networks some more. She does her job very well and is exceedingly thorough, so much so that an open post for a qualified candidate might go unfilled for months instead of weeks. The other attorneys have to add work to their plate to cover for the unfulfilled position. And, the as-yet un-hired attorney's contributions to the firm are forestalled. Ann says, "At some point, it's just not worth it to the company for me to keep going and going with my recruitment efforts. I might feel I'm moving forward but the company is really moving backwards. So now I prospect for the ten best candidates I can find in one month." Any more effort applied and the returns are diminished. Or, as a Texas professional organizer put it, "The lemonade ain't worth the squeeze."

It's tough living in the Era of Endless work. But there is a movement underway to leverage productivity gains into not only working smarter, but also working less. Jason Fried, the CEO of 37signals, a software company, has taken inspiration from the seasons and built it into the work schedule. May through October, employees work 32 hours which fits comfortably into a 4-day workweek. "We don't work the same amount of time, we work less. Better work gets done in four days than in five because we've found that when there is less time to get work done, you waste less time. In June we give everyone the chance to work on whatever they want: to explore new ideas and non-essential work. It led to a great burst of creativity."

There are efforts underway by many corporations to uncouple time from results. This makes perfect sense in the digital world of work. Instead of getting paid by the hour, you get paid for your results, and if you accomplish your results in less than five days, you're done working for the week. In the Era of Endless work it is important to create and support ideas that bring us closer to leisure. In the words of Thomas Merton in *The Ascent of Man* "... we should stop working, not for the purpose of recovering one's lost strength and becoming fit for the forthcoming labor....a Sabbath is a day for the sake of life." The sake of life. What could be more important?

---

[1]   Verizon, survey, 2010
[2]   "Working Overtime Doubles Depression Risk," CBSnews.com, January 26, 2012
[3]   Gary Small, M.D. and Gigi Vorgan, *iBrain: Surviving the Technological Alteration of the Modern Mind*
[4]   Pico Iyer, "The Joy of Quiet," *New York Times*, December 29, 2011
[5]   David Allen, *Getting Things Done*

ERA OF ENDLESS
PART
SIX

WHAT TO DO WHEN
STUFF IS ENDLESS
AND TIME IS NOT

BOOMER STUFF

In many ways, stuff has not changed. Stuff still takes time to research, price compare, decide, purchase, stow, maintain, accessorize, inventory, organize, share, charge up, replace, repair, pack, and move...to cite a few verbs. Much has already been written about how to declutter stuff. You'll find a list of helpful resources in the back of this book.

What's *new* in the Era of Endless is that Baby Boomers are about to unleash their stuff with a mighty rolling effect on Gen X and likely Gen Y. Never before has so much stuff been so problematic for so many people. Baby-boomers—millions of them—are about to unload their stuff into the landfill, thrift stores, online sales sites, storage units, and onto their children at unprecedented rates.

In the Era of Endless, Boomers are middle-aged and almost literally taking stock of their stuff. They're mentally inventorying the stuff they've accumulated over the years and coming to terms with the toll it's taking on their personal space, time, finances, and in some cases, health. In the Foreword to Ciji Ware's book, *Rightsizing Your Life,* Gail Sheehy notes that,

> "By the time we [Boomers] are moving into our Second Adulthood (midlife) we have often reached a point of exhaustion. So much effort has gone into operating the incredibly complex switches of that instrument called family life, into building careers, expanding homes, and proliferating possessions, we just want to take a deep breath. And if we allow ourselves to breathe, we'll probably feel the counter-urge to pare down, simplify, consolidate, and lighten up."[1]

If that counter-urge, or what I call the *urge to purge,* occurs at the same rate as Boomers reaching middle age, a lot of stuff is about to be unloaded! Beginning in 2010, every 60 seconds 4.4 Americans turn 50 years of age and another 3.64 turn 60. **Every minute!** It reminds me of that popular Boomer-era movie *It's a Wonderful Life* that's shown over and over again during Christmas. "Every time a bell rings it means an angel gets its wings," the film tells us. Every time a Boomers turns 50, the urge to purge gets stronger.

One driver for the dumping of stuff is that many Boomers are downsizing (or more precisely, rightsizing). The march to smaller homes is well underway. According to the Over-50 Council of the National Association of Home Builders about 6% of people between the ages of 55 and 64 move every year—so many that helping Boomers move is a growing real estate specialty industry. The exponential growth of the membership of the National Association of Senior Move Managers (NASMM) verifies the trend. Annually, NASMM helps facilitate tens of thousands of Boomers move into smaller townhouses and condos. And as if Boomer stuff was not enough, consider that the Veteran Generation, the parents of Boomers, are in their 80s and 90s. That means they will be contributing *their* stuff to the tsunami of stuff, largely by bequeathing it to Boomers.

The Crowded Nest

In the Era of Endless, the crowded nest is yet another force behind the unloading of stuff. The US census of 2010 indicates a near doubling of multi-generational living since the prior census in 2000. My client Hannah is 61. She says, "My husband was laid off in 2010. In order to make ends meet, we spent our savings, and then the savings set aside for Mother's assisted living. So she came to live with us. Getting rid of stuff to make way for her needs was paramount." Boomer home-owners facing foreclosures are moving in with family. Nearly 3.5 million brothers or sisters are living in a sibling's house. Indeed, according to the census, three generations in households is up by 30%. The empty nest may be giving way to the crowded nest, at least for some Boomers, and re-capturing personal space for multi-generational living is on the rise.

De-Acquisition Methods

It will take a wide array of de-acquisition methods to contend with all this stuff. Gratefully, in the Era of Endless there are many ways to de-acquire what Boomers, or anyone else for that matter, no longer want or need.

De-Acquisition Methods

- Donate to a brick and mortar generic charity such as the Salvation Army or Goodwill Industries.

- Donate to an online charity.

- Donate stuff to a niche charity, such as Habitat for Humanity.

- Sell stuff online.

- Auction stuff online or through public auction.

- Leave stuff at the curb for municipal waste (landfill) pick up.

- Leave stuff for people who want it free: www.freecycle.com

- Have a yard sale or garage sale. Find good tips at www.bankrate.com or www.tinyurl.com/adt988e

---

The number of yard sales and garage sales, the mother lode of used stuff, is increasing nationwide, according to www.weekendleisure.com, a website which tracks such trends. Lloyd Barton, my `client who is 58, travels the entire 654 miles through five states on Highway 127 each August during The World's Longest Yard Sale. "Everything you can imagine is for sale, but most of it looks like the stuff right out of my house," he reports. "I think we might be doing one big loop with our stuff."

You might think that buying used stuff at old-fashioned thrift stores and yard sales would be the province of Boomers, leaving online, tech-driven commerce to Gen X and Gen Y. But you'd be wrong. As of June, 2009, 21% of the unique visitors to www.craigslist.com were the over-50 crowd according to Quantcast, a company that analyzes web destinations. Marketingvox which measures the top online classified sites, claims that 15% of unique visitors are 55 or older.

Boomers are also mad for eBay, which reports 49% of all users are over the age of 50. Is the uptick due to the Boomers' penchant for a good deal on *buying* used stuff, or are Boomers *selling* their stuff? Maybe stuff is just going through one giant loop. We just don't know. But we do know stuff that keeps moving is better than stuff clogging up living spaces in homes or expensive self-storage units.

Craigslist is the fifth most visited website in the world for good reason. Craig Newmark, the founder, notes that "a culture of trust" accounts for the popularity of Craigslist. The appeal is two-fold: the thrill of turning stuff that seemingly has no cash value into surprise cash, and the satisfaction of selling to a buyer whose face you can actually see and hand you can actually shake. Trust or not, it's a good idea to follow the safety information on the Craigslist website.

As of the printing of this book the hottest sale items on Craigslist are furniture, baby gear, power tools, and sporting equipment. The hottest eBay items are cameras, computers, collectibles, jewelry, designer clothing, sports equipment, and electronics.

This Is Not Your Mother's Thrift Store

Boomers are rediscovering their local charitable thrift store as a classic, though evolving, destination for de-acquisition. I advocate for this option if you're a Boomer or the child of a Boomer in the Era of Endless. "It's an odd dynamic," Reese Jones, a Salvation Army store manager observes. "Boomers bring their stuff to the back door and get a receipt for taxes. Then they walk in the front door and shop." The sale of used stuff or what some shops call "pre-owned," (a term typically reserved for high-end products like Mercedes-Benz cars) is flourishing. "Boomers are bringing in a better quality of stuff and its paying off in higher sales" Jones says. That's good news for Goodwill Industries and the Salvation Army, nonprofits that operate over 3,500 thrift stores. They reported an increase in sales over the last five years.

The thrift store experience is much better now than in the past. True thrift stores run by bona fide charities are typically members of the Association of Resale Professionals (NARTS). NARTS sets standards of cleanliness and safety for the stores. You'll find the parking lots well-lit, the aisles well-organized, and the dressing rooms and bathrooms clean. You can also expect to run into punk rockers, costume designers, and vintage clothes collectors. Another change? Don't be surprised if your local thrift store operates an upscale boutique or specialty sections of brand name designer fashions and jewelry in their brick and mortar store, as well as online.

My Boomer client, Albert, recalls donating an "I Love Jerry Garcia" T-shirt to Goodwill. Months later he was watching former President Jimmy Carter on TV demonstrating a new water purification program in New Guinea. A young man, curious about the cameras, wandered into the background. He was wearing the exact T-shirt! In all probability it was not Albert's donated shirt, but the occurrence points out that thrift stores have gone global.

Originally started as church-operated shops to support missionaries in far off countries, thrift stores have evolved into true international retail establishments. Most of your charitable donations of clothing will not be sold in the store. Instead they are sold to third-party textile resellers called recyclers, brokers and traders. In fact, **up to 90% of donated clothes are sold to textile firms**, according to Bernard Brill of the Secondary Recycled Textiles Association. Thrift stores bundle tons of unsold clothing and sell it to brokers who pay pennies on the pound.

There's an upside and downside to this burgeoning economy. Proponents argue that the cast-off industry provides much needed jobs to workers in poor countries who handle, clean, repair, restyle, and distribute the used clothing. Opponents say the used clothing market is to blame for stunting the growth of the textile industry in some countries. Your decision to donate clothing to a thrift store is up to you, but I believe the positive aspects outnumber the negative ones.

6 Good Reasons to Donate to a Thrift Store

- Money raised in thrift stores is used to support a wide-range of social programs which may include alcohol and drug rehab, job programs, prison outreach, health care programs, programs for pregnant teens, and other worthy causes.

- Because the donations are from the public and the staff is often volunteers, the stuff can be sold at low prices to the poor and those on limited or fixed incomes.

- Second-hand stuff uses far fewer resources (gas, forests, coal, etc.) in their distribution than newly manufactured goods. When you donate used stuff you're helping the environment.

- Recycling second-hand stuff keeps it out of the landfill.

- Health care and social services programs like HIV aids testing are increasingly available at local thrift stores making these services and programs more accessible to the people who need them most, right in their com-munities.

- In exchange for your donations, you may be able to take a tax deduction on your federal income tax return.

The Skinny on Tax Deductions

You may be able to deduct fair market value of your charitable donations on your federal income tax return. The charity must have an Internal Revenue Service status as a Section 501(c)(3) organization. To determine the fair market value, visit the thrift store and check out the going rate for comparable items, or review IRS Publication 561 "Determining the Value of Donated Property" and IRS publication 526 "Charitable Deductions," both available free from www.irs.gov. Charities do not want to be responsible for determining the value of your stuff, or which items are tax deductible. That's why they give you a blank receipt for you to fill out when you drop stuff off.

When To Use Off-Site Storage

Gail Sheehy in the Foreword to the book *Rightsizing Your Life* notes,

> "...my stomach knots when I look at all the furnishings and books and chotchkes we've collected over three decades. Where to stash it all while we're in between? And once the artifacts of our life are in cold storage, will we ever have the energy to sort through it all again? To arrive at this stage still full of zest for life is an incredible gift... We have enough."[2]

Experienced professional organizers like myself can assure you that out-of-sight stuff in off-site storage is out-of-mind. The motivation to get rid of stuff that is not seen is greatly diminished, even for those with a hearty zest for life. In the Era of Endless, however, there are four circumstances when temporary off-site storage makes perfect sense.

Temporary Off-Site Storage

- The Veteran Generation—the generation that parented the Boomers—are in their late 80s and 90s. The leading edge of the Boomers will soon be entering their 70s. When there's a death in the family, sometimes the deceased's belongings need to be temporarily stored while the estate is settled. Life is not endless even if stuff is.

- A deceased's home may need to be emptied in order to sell it or pass it down.

- People transitioning to other living styles—like town-houses, condos, or smaller homes—need a temporary place for their stuff while waiting to move, especially if out of state.

- Have an exit strategy for temporary storage. Somebody needs to be thinking about a de-acquisition plan for the stuff that will not be needed in the new living situation. If that is not you, hire a professional organizer.

Hire a Professional Organizer

Call in help when you need to stage a *Mutiny of the Bounty!* A professional organizer can be invaluable in the Era of Endless when stuff seems endless and time is not. Many organizers are de-acquisition specialists who know about online and brick and mortar consignment, selling, swapping, trading, donating, auctioning, re-cycling, and good-old fashioned giving things away. For a list of professional organizers, visit www.napo.net.

E-WASTE

Electronic waste (e-waste) brings its own brand of endless. The hope is that smartphones will reduce e-waste because just one piece of equipment replaces a cell phone, camera, GPS, MP3, and other elec-tronics. But no such luck. The plethora of discarded cell phones, tablets, desktops, laptops, game consoles, and ebook readers far outweighs the technology devices the smartphone replaces. Unlike the stuff of previous generations that finds its way back to the Earth, e-waste endures for a very long time.

Obsolete electronics do not lend themselves well to donation. Goodwill alone received 23 million pounds of computers in 2006, most of them unusable and expensive to safely recycle or dispose appro-priately. Lacking a sustainable business model for re-use, or a profitable market for used parts, charities are stuck with them. Their solution is to export electronics to China, India, and Africa, using the labels of "charitable donation" and "re-usable materials program" and promises to "bridge the digital divide" to bypass e-waste prohibitions.

The Environmental Protection Agency notes that it's ten times less expensive for a company to ship e-waste overseas than to properly recycle it at home. But the health risks can be devastating. For example, eighty percent of the children in the Chinese village of Guiye suffer from lead poisoning, the direct result of exposure to toxins from separating electronic parts.

Old electronics are also sent to prison-based recycling programs where OSHA regulations are lax. This practice is likely to continue as local governments ban e-waste from their landfills.[9]

E-waste that we put in our trash is called municipal solid waste and goes to the landfill. That, too, is not a great option. Many people think landfills are designed to break down waste and turn it into harmless compost. Actually, because of the lack of moisture and air, whatever does breakdown can take over 40 years. Only 27% of plastic, metal, and glass is extracted and recycled; 16% of the waste is burned (most of that wood) and the rest, including most of the components of e-waste is simply buried.

Landfill technology is continually improving and as yet there is no reason to be alarmed. But given the dangerous chemicals with the potential to seep into ground-water or pollute the air, my philosophy is: ***reducing e-waste gives technology a chance to keep up.*** The more e-waste we can keep out of the landfill system to begin with, the more science and technology can innovate to keep us safe from its risks. What are these risks?

 ## E-Waste Risks

- Cadmium is a metal known to build up in body fat. Long-term exposure can cause lung, kidney, liver, bone, and blood damage. The largest source of cadmium is rechargeable nickel-cadmium (NiCd) batteries used in wireless phones.

- Monitors and older TVs use cathode ray tubes (CRT) which contain lead. Lead exposure can damage the nervous system, especially in small children, and is harmful to women's reproductive organs.

- Mercury is found in flat-screen monitors. Once mercury has been deposited into ground water, certain micro-organisms chemically change it into methyl mercury. This highly toxic form becomes concentrated in fish, shellfish, and animals that eat fish, making it dangerous for human consumption. Health concerns from mercury exposure include brain and nervous system damage, developmental delays, and birth defects.

- Electronics contain flame-retardants called PBDEs. Scien-tists have found that exposure to minute doses of PBDEs at critical points in development can disrupt thyroid hormones and deficits in motor skills, learning, and memory.

How Much E-Waste is There?

Some numbers are so large they make our eyes glaze over when we hear or read them, such as the national debt or the amount of money spent every year on the war in Afghanistan. The statistics surrounding e-waste are a bit like that. In 2010, the US generated 2.4 million tons of e-waste. What does that represent? 142,000 computers and 416,000 mobile devices **a day!** You can check with www.etakeback.org for a continual update on the numbers.

Desktop computers, printers, keyboards, and televisions lead the way with mobile devices, laptops, and tablets adding to e-waste every day. The important thing to remember is even as landfill and recycling technologies improve, *reduction* is always the best course of action.

Longevity is not the only endless quality of e-waste. With a seemingly endless stream of new versions, models, and editions of electronic and digital products, obsolescence comes so quickly it's often easier, faster, and cheaper to simply keep the stuff as relics rather than safely recycle or otherwise de-acquire them. Planned obsolescence is not new. For nearly 75 years, manufacturers have been producing products that become less useful or non-functional in a defined time frame. Light bulbs are a good example. Even Walmart buildings are intentionally designed to last only 25 years.

The upside of planned obsolescence is that it drives innovation. Replacing old TVs with digital televisions is a good example. Planned obsolescence fuels economic growth and protects consumers from faulty products. The downside is that continuous replacement rather than repair uses more energy and creates more waste. The two con-sumer items least practical to repair are computers and cell phones. These are precisely the same consumables that are nearly impossible to break down in a landfill.

Planted Obsolescence

A newer kind of obsolescence is at play in the Era of Endless stuff. I call it *planted* obsolescence. Young acquirers with many consuming years ahead of them, embrace the *predictable* replacement of electronic, computerized, or digital products of their generation. Unlike planned obsolescence built into the product, this new kind of obsolescence is planted in the acquirer by the messaging of marketers, manufacturers, and peer culture. The message is that a product becomes obsolete when a newer version, edition, or model becomes available. Or, it becomes uncool, a much more psychological construct.

Social network shopping is making acquirers out of more and more young people. Based on the principles of the wisdom of the crowd, large groups of peer users recommend products to each other. We can expect social network shopping to be a driver in planted obsolescence well into the future.

Do You Really Need a New Device?

In the spirit of reduction, think twice before you buy a new device. You want one, you know you do. And that's fine. But if you want to take a more measured approach and assess if you actually *need* a new device, there are some guidelines.

You might not realize how much your current devices can do. I have a client who needed a talking alarm and didn't realize her existing smartphone had one. Not only could it ring, but it could verbalize the time. Did you know, if you hold down the main button on your iPhone, you can activate voice control? Voice control allows you to command the phone to dial a person loaded in your Contacts, a great feature if you're driving.

Learn What Your Current Tools Can Do

- Watch a tutorial.
- Read the manual.
- See YouTube videos.
- Play with your technology tools just for the fun of it to learn what they can do.
- Visit www.makeuseof.com and www.lifehacker.com, useful websites with how-to guides for just about everything.
- Read online reviews from professional sources. For electronics, my clients recommend www.pcmag.com, www.cnet.com, and www.gizmodo.com for unbiased, easy-to-understand information.
- Follow user reviews posted on www.amazon.com, a reliable source; round out your research by visiting www.bizrate.com or www.consumerreview.com.
- Use Facebook and other social media for recommendations from family and friends.

Designate a Device Captain

Electronic stuff is here to stay but you exert some control on it by designating a Device Captain in your family. The Device Captain takes responsibility for the electronic stuff. It's a perfect chore for a digital native teen or young adult. For instance, my client's 15 year old daughter is the Device Captain in her house. She keeps all the devices synced, makes sure they're charged, labels all the accessories and cords, and downloads updates, patches and fixes. And most of all, she takes out the garbage, in this case old devices for recycling, donating or selling.

Alternatives to Landfill and Thrift Store Donation

Sell/Re-use. By bringing millions of buyers and sellers together, the eBay marketplace, and other websites like it, enable reuse on a large scale. Reusing computers, cell phones, and electronics extends their useful life. This maximizes thei-r value before they're finally recycled. It also delays their entry into the waste stream as we wait for technological advances in recycling techniques. More information can be found at www.ecosquid.com and www.rethink.ebay.com.

Buy-Back Programs. Buy from manufacturers, such as Sony, who offer buy-back programs. Sony promises to take back, at no charge, electronics, even older ones, and recycle them in the US via a network of national collection locations. Go to www.computertakeback.com, the Electronics Take-Back Coalition's website.

Pressure your Congressperson to support ethical recycling practices such as no dumping of toxic e-waste in developing countries, no use of prison labor for recycling, and no disposal in landfills.

Bring your stuff to a Responsible Recycler in the E-Steward Program. They'll repair and donate your electronics for charity. If your device is beyond repair, they'll extract the valuable metals in the US rather than using child labor overseas. Find a Responsible Recycler at www.e-stewards.org

Practice Hand-Me-Ups. Whenever you acquire a new technology toy, tool or device, give the older version to a friend or family member.

---

[1]   Ciji Ware, *Rightsizing Your Life*. Foreword by Gail Sheehy
[2]   Gail Sheehy

RESOURCES FOR GETTING ORGANIZED IN THE ERA OF ENDLESS

Books

Allen Elkin, *How to Get Rid of Clutter for Dummies*

Ciji Ware, *Rightsizing Your Life: Simplifying Your Surroundings While Keeping What Matters Most*

David Allen, *Getting Things Done*

David Weinberger, *Too Big to Know: Rethinking Knowledge*

Evan Carroll and John Romano, *Your Digital Afterlife*

Francis Wade, *Bill's Imperfect Time Management Adventure*

Gary Small, MD, *iBrain: Surviving the Technological Alteration of the Modern Mind*

Institute for Challenging Disorganization, *Guide to Challenging Disorganization for Professional Organizers*

Judith Kolberg, various books and reports at www.squallpress.net

Julie Hall, *The Boomers Burden: Dealing with Your Parent's Lifetime Accumulation of Stuff*

Julie Morgenstern, *Organizing From the Inside Out*

Larry Rosen, *iDisorder: Understanding Our Obsession with Technology and Overcoming Its Hold on Us*

Melissa Mannon, *Unofficial Family Archivist*

Regina Lark, *Psychic Debris, Crowded Closets: The Relationship Between the Stuff in Your Head and What's Under the Bed*

Steven Covey, *The 7 Habits of Highly Successful People*

Susan Cain, *Quiet: The Power of Introvertism in a World That Can't Stop Talking*

Valorie Burton, *How Did I Get So Busy*

Viktor Mayer-Schonberger, *Delete: The Virtue of Forgetting in the Digital Age*

William Powers, *Hamlet's Blackberry*

Websites

www.1Calendar.com

www.2time-sys.com

www.amazon.com

www.bankrate.com

www.bizrate.com

www.businessinsider.com/best-productivity-apps-2012-2012-12?op=1

www.cert.org

www.cnet.com

www.computertakeback.com

www.consumerreview.com

www.Coolendar.com

www.craigslist.com

www.deleteme.com

www.delicious.com

www.dropbox.com

www.ecosquid.com

www.e-stewards.org

www.etakeback.org

www.freecycle.com

www.gizmodo.com

www.irs.gov

www.juliemorgenstern.com

www.justorganizeyourstuff.com

www.lifehacker.com

www.makeuseof.com

www.mckinseyquarter.com (research)

www.mindtools.com

www.mint.com

www.pcmag.com

www.pewInternet.org (research)

www.practicalhacks.com

www.reqall.com

www.rethink.ebay.com

www.retrevo.com

www.squidoo.com
www.stumbleupon.com
www.usa.gov.
www.virtualassistants.com
www.web.mit.edu/tac (research)
www.webecoist.com
www.weekendleisure.com
www.YouMail.com
www.zhornsoftware.co.uk/stickies/

Helpful Organizations

Association of Senior Move Managers, www.nasmm.org

Fileheads Professional Organizers, www.fileheads.net

Institute for Challenging Disorganization,
   www.challengingdisorganization.org

National Association of Professional Organizers, www.napo.net

Getting Organized in the Era of Endless

INDEX

digital sticky notes, 95
Direct Marketing Association, 21
directions, 2, 44, 95, 113
disaster preparedness, 110, 111, 113
discretionary time, 52
disposables, 29, 57
distracted, 23, 24, 92
dividing your attention, 91
document, 15, 17, 18, 20, 27, 40, 45,
  51, 56, 66, 71, 75, 76, 77, 79, 80, 82,
  84, 85, 86
domain name, 84
done, xiii, 1, 7, 11, 21, 31, 42, 43, 47,
  49, 51, 55, 63, 64, 66, 67, 68, 69, 93,
  102, 103, 111, 116, 117
dopamine, 42, 51, 97n4
download, 39, 45, 52, 82, 93, 132
downsize, 33, 56
driver distraction, 96
due date, 68, 112
Dunbar, R.I.M., 35n1
DVD, 79

E

ease of use, 10
eat, 8, 9, 79, 129
eBay, 27, 34, 124, 132
e-books, 42
economize, 7, 8, 9, 19, 25, 34, 71, 80
economizer, 8, 23
economy of time, 7, 13
economy, 7, 13, 17, 125
effect, 7, 20, 21, 22, 33, 48, 53, 58, 73,
  96, 101, 110, 111, 113, 121
effective, 11, 90, 111
effective, use of time, 2, 111
effectiveness, 116
efficiency expert, 10
efficiency, 16, 17, 19, 20, 31, 46, 108
efficient, 7, 8, 18, 25, 32, 48, 70
efficient, use of time, 2, 8
effort, 7, 19, 20, 33, 42, 47, 48, 71, 73,
  78, 90, 101, 110, 113, 116, 121
Egyptian, 12
Einstein, Albert, 40
electronic information, 133
electronic mail, 31. *See also* email
electronic waste, 128-130. *See also* e-
  waste
Electronics Take-Back Coalition, 133
electronics, 56, 57, 124, 128, 130, 132,
  133
email, 3, 31, 33, 39, 40, 44, 45, 47, 48,
  50, 52, 53, 69, 70, 71, 74, 76, 80, 82,
  84, 86, 93, 94, 95, 101, 102, 104,
  105, 106, 107, 111
embodied interaction, 33
emotions, 111
endless connectedness, 51, 105
endless distractions, 2, 39, 46, 47, 90
endless information, 39-46, 61-86
endless interruption, 46-47, 87-97
endless stuff, 56-57, 119-133
endless work, 47-52, 99-117
energy, 33, 102, 103, 109, 111, 127,
  130
entertainment, 3, 14, 96, 107
environment, 1, 12, 26, 45, 51, 92, 93,
  117, 126
Environmental Protection Agency, 128
Era of Endless information, 39-46, 61-
  86
Era of Endless interruption, 46-47, 87-
  97
Era of Endless stuff, 56-57, 119-133
Era of Endless work, 47-52, 99-117
Era of Endless, 37-58
errands, 23, 44, 70, 94
estate, 85, 127
E-Steward Program, 133
ethno-archeological study, 56
Evernote, 65, 109
e-waste risks, 129
e-waste, 128-130, 133. *See also*
  electronic waste.
Excel, 77
excellence, 91
excess, 16, 28, 52, 73, 74, 90
executive function, 95
executor, 56, 85
exercise, 28, 42, 76, 78, 93, 94, 105
exit strategy, 127
expectation, 24, 48, 50, 70, 107, 108
Expedia, 103
expiration date, 74

F

F&P, 73, 74. *See also* Filtering and
  Purging
Facebook, 49, 51, 56, 81, 93, 96, 104,
  105, 106, 132
FaceTime, 55, 56, 103
factories, 15, 17
factory workers, 19
facts, 43, 63, 66
Fake, Caterina, 58n2
family archives, 86
family dinners, 48, 102, 105

56, 58, 73, 76, 81, 82, 83, 111, 112, 113
output, 19, 30, 74, 81, 82
Over-50 Council, 122
over-commitment, 113
over-stimulated, 64
overtime, 30, 48, 101
Owens, Jesse, 25

P

paper, 10, 26, 32, 33, 40, 41, 42, 44, 79, 80, 85
paperless office, 41
papers 17, 18, 77, 79, 96
parents, 28, 45, 55, 56, 96, 108, 122
Pareto Principle, 19
Pareto, Vilfredo, 19
passage of time, 11
password, 44, 56, 84, 85, 109
PBDEs, 130
pcmag, 109, 132
PDA, 33. *See also* personal digital assistant
peer culture, 131
pen, 33, 40
personal days, 103
personal digital assistant, 33. *See also* PDA
personal information, 77
personal papers, 77
personal productivity, 48, 102
Pew Internet Report, 69
phone, 26, 31, 33, 47, 55, 57, 69, 70, 79, 80, 92, 93, 94, 95, 101, 102, 106, 108, 111, 128, 129, 130, 131, 132. *See also* telephone
photos, 3, 45, 49, 51, 52, 82, 83, 85, 86, 95, 103
plan, 11, 20, 29, 33, 34, 50, 54, 84, 909, 83, 101, 103, 104, 106, 111, 127
planned obsolescence, 130, 131
Planning Imperative in Human Behavior, The, 11
planning, 11, 12, 32, 34, 47, 55, 84, 92
planted obsolescence, 131
Pliny the Elder, 13
Pocket Planner, 32, 33
podcast, 42, 86
pointer, 67
Polley, Eugene, 25
POP, 46, 49, 51, 89.
positive side to interruption, 89, 90
possessions, 28, 56, 76, 121
possibility, 46, 85, 89, 90

post office, 15, 23
Post-it notes, 27, 47, 95
potential, 46, 58, 89
Potential/Opportunity/Possibility, *See* POP
Powers, William, 41, 75
Practical Hacks, 70
predict, 54, 74, 103
predictable, 131
predicted, 47
prevention, 113, 114
Principles of Scientific Management, 19
principles of scientific management, 20
print, 27, 41, 55, 82, 85
printer, 29, 39, 40, 41, 44, 80, 130
printing press, 14
printing, 14, 32, 40, 84, 102, 124
priorities, 10, 31, 49, 109, 112, 113
privacy, 49, 79, 91
problem-solving, 76, 104
processes, 20, 30
productivity, 19, 21, 30, 31, 47, 48, 49, 101, 102, 104, 107, 108, 109, 111, 114, 116
productivity, personal, 48, 102
professional organizers, 1, 2, 28, 30, 75, 76, 77, 127, 128.
project management, 32, 94
project, 34, 58, 69, 103, 11
projects, 21, 22, 31, 49, 50, 54, 82, 92, 110
prosperity, 22, 23, 26, 28
Protestant Ethic and the Spirit of Capitalism, The, 17
Protestant work ethic, 14, 17, 21
Publick Occurrences Both Forreign and Domestick, 14
pull-back, 54, 65, 66
purge, 81, 83, 121, 122
purging, 73, 74, 75, 82, 83
purging-by-output, 74, 82
"Pursuit of Useless Information, The", 58n4

Q

qualitatively, 67
quality of life, 1, 2, 10, 12, 17, 23, 30, 32, 39, 50, 64, 109, 113
Quantcast, 123
quantitative, 68
QuickBooks, 80
Quiet: The Power of Introverts in a World That Can't Stop Talking, 91